HELPING FAMILIES IN DISTRESS
An Introduction to Family Focused Helping

ABOUT THE AUTHORS

Stephen Murgatroyd is 34 years old and holds degrees from University College Cardiff and the Open University. A counselling psychologist, he has contributed over 60 papers to the psychology literature. His books include *Helping the Troubled Child – Interprofessional Case Studies* (Harper and Row, 1980) and *Coping with Crisis* (Harper and Row, 1982) – the latter text co-authored with Ray Woolfe. He is currently the Associate Editor of the *British Journal of Guidance and Counselling* and is a former editor of *The Counsellor*. He has offered counsellor training programmes in England, Wales, Canada, the USA and Norway. He is married and has two children.

Ray Woolfe is 43 years old and is married with two children. He has worked for the past 12 years for the Open University's School of Education. He has participated widely in counselling training programmes both in Britain and abroad and has considerable experience in working in groups with a variety of adults. He is a member of the Executive Committee of the Counselling Section of the British Psychological Society and is a practising marriage guidance counsellor. His other publications include *Coping with Crisis* (Harper and Row, 1982) with Stephen Murgatroyd; *Learning in Groups: A Humanistic Perspective* (Open University, 1984) and *Personal Change in Adults* (Open University, 1981) with Ken Giles.

HELPING FAMILIES IN DISTRESS
An Introduction to Family Focused Helping

Stephen Murgatroyd
The Open University in Wales
and
The University College, Cardiff

and

Ray Woolfe
The Open University

Harper & Row, Publishers
London

Cambridge
Philadelphia
New York
San Francisco

Mexico City
São Paulo
Singapore
Sydney

Copyright © 1985 Stephen Murgatroyd and Ray Woolfe
All rights reserved
First published 1985

Harper & Row Ltd
28 Tavistock Street
London WC2E 7PN

No part of this book may be reproduced in any manner whatsoever without written permission, except in the case of brief quotations embodied in critical articles and reviews.

British Library Cataloguing in Publication Data
Murgatroyd, Stephen
　Helping families in distress: an introduction to family focused helping.
　　1. Family social work　　2. Family psychotherapy
　I. Title　　II. Woolfe, Ray
　362.8′286　　HV 697

ISBN 0-06-318316-1

Typeset by S & S Press, Abingdon, Oxfordshire
Printed and bound by Butler and Tanner Ltd, Frome and London

CONTENTS

About the Authors
Acknowledgements
Preface

1	The Focus for Helping	1
2	How do Families Create Distress?	15
3	Rules, Roles and Boundaries – Helping and Family Communications	33
4	Transference, Projection and Insight – Features of the Psychoanalytic Tradition	64
5	Modifying Behaviour and Promoting 'Family Life Skills'	85

6	The Role of a Helper in a Family Crisis	118
7	Problems in Helping Families	138
	References	155
	Index	165

This book is dedicated to

Lynne, James and Glyn Murgatroyd,
to the memory of Teresa Leclerc

and to
Adrienne, Alexander and Clare Woolfe

ACKNOWLEDGEMENTS

The writing of a book of this kind involves many contributing to the shaping of the ideas that inform it. It is not possible to acknowledge fully all those who have contributed in this way. However, we do wish to thank our colleagues in the Coping with Crisis Research Group at the Open University – Sylvia Rhys, Mike Shooter, Tony Hobbs, Gill Fitzgibbon, Camilla Lambert – and those who have participated in this group's training events, for their continued support.

In the preparation of the manuscript the following have played various parts: Sandra Bewick, Gill Monkley, Sue Thomas and especially Christine Horner. Their work has made this project possible.

In addition we would like to thank the following individuals for specific contributions to our thinking: Brian Cade, Mike Apter, Paul Brown and Linda Berman. As always the final responsibility for this text is ours alone.

Finally, Naomi Roth at Harper and Row continues to show faith in our work – a fact for which we are grateful.

Stephen Murgatroyd
Ray Woolfe

PREFACE

In 1982 Harper and Row published our text *Coping with Crisis*, which represented the product of our work over a three-year period with the Coping with Crisis Research and Training Group of the Open University. This last book was oriented towards work with individuals both alone and in group settings and, though it contained a chapter on divorce and separation, its orientation towards the family was limited. The present text, based on continuation of our earlier work, is allied to our growing interest and involvement in helping families, and aims to fill the gap evident in that earlier work.

The book does not purport to be a textbook on family therapy. While we hope it will be of interest to specialist family therapists, our intention is that the content should be accessible, relevant and illuminating to a much wider audience. Accordingly we make no attempt to provide a comprehensive review of all the different perspectives currently available. Nor would we claim to offer an exhaustive account of any single school of thought. Rather we seek to offer readers a taster of what is available or (to change the metaphor) to allow readers to 'dip their feet in the water' and see how it feels. Our contention is that many helpers, ostensibly working alone with individuals, are in fact already adopting a family focus for their work, sometimes without being aware that they are doing so. We hope to help such readers to become more aware of the issues involved in this work and to increase the choices available to them, as well as outlining some boundaries and limitations. We have tried to integrate theory and practice in a way which avoids the Scylla of detailing bodies of theory which seem to be far removed from actual practices and the Charybdis of describing practices which seem to form a *pot-pourri*, around which it is difficult to see any underlying conceptual structure. We hope that through the judicious use of case illustration and example, we have succeeded in demonstrating the links between theory and practice in the work of helpers, whatever their professional standing or background.

So far as our own theoretical position and value judgements are concerned, these can be broadly defined as both humanistic and pragmatic. They are pragmatic in two senses. First, we have no exclusive commitment to a particular theory or methodology. While we naturally favour some approaches rather than others, we have tried in this book to demonstrate the pragmatic and eclectic nature of much that counts as helping people. Helpers often draw on a variety of theories in their day to day practices and we have tried to make this explicit in the course of the book, especially in our use of case illustration. Secondly, we would describe ourselves as pragmatists in the sense that we readily acknowledge that many of the problems of families in distress are structural or economic in origin and we do not wish to deny this 'fact' nor to suggest that people's attitudes, feelings and relationships are not rooted in a powerfully defining ideological structure. Indeed we hope our commitment to political change and to working at the level of community action is clearly and unambiguously expressed in this book, as it was in *Coping with Crisis* (Woolfe, 1983). At the same time, we think that helpers can intervene in a realistic, non-utopian way to assist individuals and families to cope with distress in the present and to increase their potential to influence the world in which they live. (For a discussion of the dilemmas involved in this position, see Leonard, 1984.)

We hope that reading this book, will enable helpers to do five things: (a) to understand better the nature of distress in families; (b) to examine different strategies and tactics for helping families; (c) to explore the psychology and social psychology of helping families; (d) to understand more fully the social limits to helping families; (e) to examine a limited number of specific cases of family helping in detail.

Some readers of this book will unarguably be working with families – the obvious examples are family therapists based in institutions like the Tavistock Clinic, the Institute of Psychiatry (both in London) and the Family Institutes in London and Cardiff. But for many readers, the relevance of a family approach may at first sight appear less explicit. We would like to address this issue directly. As we point out in detail in the first chapter, the family is more than the sum of its individual parts; families have their own dynamics and the 'needs' presented by an individual member reflect the nature of this dynamic, which consists of rules and forms of communication and interaction. As soon as a helper begins to consider the needs of an individual in such a context, then he or she is starting to engage in family focused helping. One does not need to be seeing all or even more than one member of a family to make this statement valid. If the orientation of the helper's work is to look at the individual in such a way, then family focused therapy or helping is a feature of what is taking place. We would contend that a high percentage of those persons involved in counselling and therapeutic work with individuals adopt precisely such a stance (although not necessarily all the time) and that, consciously or unconsciously, helpers are engaging in forms of family focused helping. A few examples of how different helpers become involved in family focused work might be helpful here.

The *marriage guidance counsellor* sees people as individuals or sees couples; some of the issues that arise (e.g. the effect of having children upon the marital relationship; the effect of children leaving home upon the relationship; the way in which family relationships as a whole operate) are clearly family focused and prove important components in understanding the nature and form of the marital relationship between the couple.

Clinical psychologists may see maladjusted children on their own or sometimes with their parents but nearly all would now recognize the need to try to understand the child's behaviour in its family context and not as an isolated individual acting outside the influence of family relationships. They look at how that behaviour derives from this setting and how it may express the emotional needs of the child and of other family members.

Community nurses and *health visitors* spend some of their time with young mothers who are lonely and isolated and whose own emotional needs are often manifest in the treatment of their children. But these needs are often basically a reflection of underlying problems with their husbands or their own parents that may never have been resolved. Increasingly community nurses and health visitors have become workers with families, not just with mothers.

Doctors treat a great many people for depression or sleeplessness by chemotherapy, but the depression or sleeplessness perhaps hides underlying feelings of anger or fear which the patient's relationships within the family do not allow him or her to express. Many doctors now try to offer a counselling role as part of their work.

Social workers have to cope with a great many difficulties, including the problem of child battering, knowing full well that removing a child from home may do little to resolve more fundamental issues about dissatisfaction with life and inability to cope with stress or difficult personal relationships.

Many professionals are only too well aware of the limitation inherent in a nonholistic approach to people, concentrating on treating symptoms rather than causes, and they are highly sensitive to the importance of the social, community and family networks in which their clients operate. To such helpers we hope that this book will widen the range of options and interpretations available. To helpers who are perhaps less well aware of underlying family relationships and dynamics, we hope that this book will open up a number of possibilities which will increase their understanding, effectiveness and satisfaction with their work.

The structure of the book reflects the hopes, aspirations and objectives we have outlined above. The initial chapter is concerned to elaborate the point already made, namely that the family is a relevant focus for much that passes as helping in our society. This is followed by a chapter which seeks to place distress into some kind of social, economic and cultural perspective by considering the question, how do families cause distress? In an early plan for the book this was to be followed by a series of chapters on different theoretical perspectives. As we have worked on this writing project we gradually modified these initial ideas so as to acknowledge the fact that our audience is *not* primarily a body of specialist family therapists. So while we do include chapters on the psychoanalytical and behaviouristic approaches respectively, we do so less for the purpose of providing a comprehensive account of these perspectives, than to offer readers an insight into how such perspectives may already or could potentially be reflected in their own work. The original plan had also contained chapters on the more substantive contemporary approaches to the field of family therapy such as the structural approach, the strategic approach, the use of paradox, the Milan school, etc. While we have tried to provide an account of some of these perspectives, we have sought to do so in a form which seeks to help readers to an awareness of what they each have to say about the underlying dynamics of family life rather than to present a detailed account of each theoretical position which is complete and thoroughgoing in itself. The result of this shift in focus is reflected in Chapter 3 on 'Rules, Roles and Boundaries', which gives a combined account of some of these contemporary, more specialized and perhaps less familiar approaches. This is followed by the chapters on psychoanalysis and behaviourism. We then provide a chapter on crisis work with features which point to the crisis-oriented nature of much of the work undertaken by helpers in our society. We are concerned in this chapter to demonstrate the ways in which crisis work differs from longer-term approaches to helping. In a final chapter we offer readers an account of some practical problems faced by helpers in the day to day nuts and bolts of helping.

Two points need to be clear from the beginning of this book. The first concerns our assumptions about the helping process. Throughout this book a variety of helping techniques and processes are described. For example, the chapter which deals with rules, roles and boundaries (Chapter 3) briefly describes the techniques used in some aspects of strategic family focused work and a whole array of procedures are documented in the chapter on behaviourism (Chapter 5). The successful use of these procedures and processes is, whatever the circumstances, dependent upon the quality of the helper's relationships with the individuals and the family with whom they are working. This relationship will need to involve: (a) a sensitivity on the part of the helper to the feelings and concerns of the family – this sensitivity will determine both the nature and pace of the helping process; (b) the helper explaining to the family members with whom he or she is working the rationale for the procedures used so that they do not feel manipulated, used or exploited; (c) the helper seeking to build trust and show concern both between him- or herself and the family members and also between the family members themselves; (d) the helper being genuine in his or her transactions with those whom he or she seeks to help – he or she should not be 'role-playing' the role of helper; (e) the helper needing to be 'concrete' – meaning that he or she should be seen to be working with the specific problems and concerns of the family, and finally (f) the helper needing to show warmth and empathy to those who seek his or her help. This is a long list. It really implies that helpers need to 'be' rather than 'do' when they are helping – they need to share their 'self' with those they are helping (Hill, 1958). Given these observations, the descriptions of helping processes we provide in the chapters which follow are dry and over-logical. In fact, the helping process is complex, difficult and challenging. In reading these process descriptions it is important to bear these basic points in mind.

The second general point we need to make at the outset concerns terminology. At various points in this book we attend to the way in which helpers working within various traditions choose to describe both themselves and those they are seeking to help. Terms helpers use for themselves include 'counsellor', 'advisor', 'therapist'; terms helpers use for those they seek to help include 'client', 'patient', 'punter', 'person in need'. Each of these terms carries implicit values and ideological assumptions – a point discussed at appropriate junctures in this text. Unless quoting from some other source, we have maintained the term of 'helper' to describe all those counsellors, advisors and therapists to whom this book is addressed. In part this is because we have a commitment to demystifying and making accessible ideas and processes between professional and para-professional groups and in part because helping seems to us to embrace more accurately the spirit of this text. Our term for the individual, subgroup or family seeking help is usually 'family' or 'person in need'. Our hope is that these terms will not be off-putting to readers more familiar with other terms and that our deliberate use of these terms will indeed encourage some degree of demystification.

This book is as much about us as it is about helping families. It reflects our commitment to understanding complex human processes within some kind of structured framework. It also reflects our concern to ensure that those processes are located securely in their social structure and that helping families is not seen as divorced from this structure. In writing it, we have come to understand these processes more clearly. We hope that this may also be your experience in reading it.

July 1984

Stephen Murgatroyd,
Cardiff

Ray Woolfe,
Manchester

1

THE FOCUS FOR HELPING

Introduction

Social workers, clinical psychologists, resettlement workers, educational psychologists and others often speak of their work in terms of their 'clients' or 'cases': by this they usually mean individuals. Others, such as doctors and psychiatrists, speak of 'patients', by which they also mean individuals. When clients, cases or patients are being described the unit of measurement is the person who is seen to be in some need. Such workers speak of the needs of individuals in a variety of ways. For example, school counsellors speak of needs in terms of educational needs (i.e. concept development, learning potential), personal needs (i.e. to develop social skills) and vocational needs (i.e. to make and plan career choices). Others see needs in terms of transitional needs, developmental needs, crisis- or stress-related needs or needs in terms of self-development. In all these need descriptions the unit upon which the helper is focusing is the individual client. Indeed, there is a school of counselling and helping known as 'client-centred' or 'person-centred' (Rogers, 1957) and a great many forms of helping intervention which are individually oriented. Case studies of the person in need and of helping and counselling are also widely available (i.e. Eysenck, 1976; Murgatroyd, 1980).

Individualizing Need

This individualizing of need has a variety of roots. First, it ties in strongly with our notions of illness. We are used to thinking of such illnesses as ischaemic heart disease or cancer as residing in an individual and creating for that individual a need for treatment. We are not used to thinking of heart disease as (in part at least) a function of the society's failure to discourage smoking, to promote effective health education and to encourage and enable exercise so as to reduce obesity. Yet this last explanation of heart disease risk factors is as convincing as an explanation that sees the individual patient as the beginning and end of the definition of need. One consequence of the individualizing of need in the case of heart disease, just to stay with this example for a moment, is that substantial sums of money are being spent on individual drug treatments to reduce high blood pressure at a time when equally substantial amounts of money are being spent promoting cigarette advertising. Both smoking and high blood pressure are known risk factors in heart disease. To treat one symptom (blood pressure) and not another (the ecouragement to smoke) shows the effect of individualizing need.

This relates to a much broader point, described especially clearly in Cochrane (1972). It is that, when policies concerned with promoting health are being considered, it is generally the case that much more attention is focused upon doctor–patient relationships and the provision of individual patient facilities (i.e. expensive coronary care units) than upon the social policies which, if implemented, could reduce illness. Cochrane argues, convincingly, that mortality rates are more affected by changes in social policy (especially in relation to the treatment of sewage, the planning of housing and the promotion of sanitation within dwellings via improvement grants) than by the intervention of helpers defining the problems in individual terms. The medical model, and its substantial support in the economy, can be regarded in particular cases to be a threat to health (Illich, 1972) where health is defined as community well-being rather than the well-being of a particular patient. Despite these kinds of observations, the notion of need in illness being individualized has been a powerful shaper of need definition in all helping professions.

Another powerful notion relates to the nature of a person's psychological well-being. It is interesting that psychologists and others have often adopted the same terminology as doctors when describing the basic processes they use. For example, people are referred to as patients. The problems which such people present are sometimes referred to as symptoms (either neurotic or psychotic *symptoms*) and the term 'treatment strategy' or 'treatment intervention' is used to describe the actions which the psychologists take when working with a person in need. The unit of attention is the patient's 'needs' as identified in some symptom. The action of the helper here is related to the removal of the symptoms causing psychological distress so as to return that person to 'psychological health'. The medical model of the nature of psychological distress individualizes the problem a person presents and provides a powerful model for intervention. Some psychologists have sought to overcome this difficulty by the use of the term 'client' instead of 'patient' and by calling themselves 'counsellors' rather than 'therapists'. In some cases these changes of nomenclature are cosmetic. In most cases, however, these changes of descriptive terms imply a change in ideological position. 'Clients' do not have 'symptoms' – but they are deficient in some way (hence the need for 'social skills' or 'assertiveness' or 'personal growth'); 'counsellors' do not pretend to the professionalism and medicalism of the 'therapist', but the term does imply a professional position above that of helper or befriender or priest. Paul Halmos (1965) describes such changes of language as typifying the acts of faith which the new psychology is seeking to embody in its attempt to replace the old ideology of the medical model. In doing so, the new language perpetuates some of the assumptions of the medical model – most especially assumptions about the nature of the power relationship between counsellor and client.

This individualizing of need amongst the so-called psychosocial helping professions (as opposed to the medical professions) also has another root: the nature of psychology itself. As several writers have observed (Adlam *et al.*, 1976; Woolfe, 1983; Leonard, 1984), psychology generally sees the person as a free agent able to exercise rational choices in a free world where equality is protected by the State. This is essentially a capitalist notion of psychology (and therefore of helping founded upon psychological interventions), where 'free markets' of 'individual choice' are seen to be the basis of need statements. Whilst it is true that psychologists also accept the principle that 'weak members' of society ought to be protected from the exercise of power by the strong – hence special provision for mentally handicapped and physically handicapped people – it is equally true that the definitions of weakness and strength are individualized in terms of personal deficits. Thus women are seen to be equal to men unless they have individual deficits (i.e. a physical disability or a special educational need), whereas it is patently clear that women are not equal to men in terms of social opportunity. Psychological well-being or disturbance is thus defined in psychology in terms of the person not being able to function effectively in the world of free choice, irrespective of his or her membership of groups who are socially disadvantaged. This is especially clear in the case of behaviour therapy (see Erwin, 1973) and those psychological therapies which promote 'self-actualization' (i.e. May, 1967; Perls, 1969). Needs are again individualized in a broad framework of a society of real individual choice.

A different reason for helpers and counsellors seeing the individual as the 'unit' for helping concerns effectiveness and efficiency. It is difficult to assess the psychological and social needs of a person, but it is even more difficult to assess the psychological needs of a family or a community or a network of people. Individual assessment, though difficult, is generally thought to be more accurate than assessment of large groups. In just the same way, therapeutic intervention is often thought of as being more tailored to needs when delivered on a one to one basis than in a group. Finally, the outcome of some intervention is thought to be accurately assessible for a single person – more so than for a category of persons. Thus many helping professionals prefer working on a one to one basis since they feel that they are more able to tune their skills and assess development at this level than at the level of, say, a family *in toto* or a community. Whilst there is little empirical evidence to support the view that helping in groups or through community development is inherently more demanding or stressful than working with individuals, the belief and feeling that it is, is enough to deter many helpers from attempting group work, family focused helping or community development.

This leads to a final reason for seeing needs in individual terms. It is that helpers, though often investing considerable energy in a concern for their 'clients', are concerned about their own needs. Many report (e.g. Boy and Pine, 1980) that working with more than one person at a time creates more demands upon their personal resources and skills than does working with individuals. Others suggest that burn-out is greater when the helper is working as a member of a team with a group than when he or she is working on a one to one basis. Burn-out is reduced when the helper feels most in control of a situation and, for many, this occurs when the relationship he or she has with 'clients' is on a one to one basis.

This section has outlined a number of different reasons for helping professionals and counsellors to regard needs as residing with individuals. The prevalence of the medical model, the construction of helping roles around the notion of personal deficits and symptoms, the dominantly capitalist notions of psychological health, and the needs of helpers to avoid burn-out and feel able to assess, monitor, evaluate and control their work are all powerful reasons for helping to be seen in terms of an individual's need. These features of helping have a long history and are well established, both in terms of the codes of ethics agreed for doctors, nurses, social workers, counsellors, psychotherapists and others and in terms of the way in which many helping organizations are structured. The individual is clearly the focus for a great deal of helper attention.

Given these observations, it is interesting that two clearly established levels at which a helper can choose to intervene – the family or the community – have emerged in the last two decades as powerful alternatives to the individualized construction of both need and helping. Whilst these two alternative points of focus for helping have not led to the abandonment of some of the features outlined above, their focus *is* sufficiently different to provide a radical departure in terms of the conception of need and in terms of the nature of helping processes.

The Family Focus

Family focused helping – known more generally as family therapy – begins with a different set of assumptions about the construction of need than that used in one to one, individualized helping. It does not take the individual as the unit for intervention but rather seeks to affect the nature of the family as a whole. Clearly, individual family members do contribute in unique and important ways to the families of which they are part and they do help to shape the relationships and experiences within them. But the family is more than the sum of these individual contributions: families have their own dynamics, their own structures and strategies and their own 'games' by which the contributions of the individuals within the family are mediated. That is, the actions and experiences of individuals within the family are a function of and derive from the way the family operates. Thus the 'needs' presented by an individual within a family arise from the nature of the family's communication and interactions systems and it is this that the helper needs to focus upon if he or she is to reduce the distress within the family.

An analogy from physics is often useful to elaborate the point just made. The physicist, when studying a particular substance, chooses between two levels when analysing that substance: the atom or molecule as the unit of study (equivalent here to the individual) or the nature of the substance as a compound (equivalent here to the family dynamics). Both units of focus have their own traditions and assumptions, but they provide very different levels of interpretation for the study of substances.

In helping the two levels so far introduced here are the individual (atom or molecule) and the family (compound). The core assumption of working with the individual is that there is a need to understand and affect that person's psychology, social support and social skills; in helping at the level of the family the core assumption is that there is a need to understand and affect the interactions between individuals who are members of a family system. This highlights a further device for differentiating between individual and family approaches to helping, namely the difference between 'within-person' helping (individual) and 'between-person' helping (family).

The distinction between individual and family focused helping is more than a difference of nomenclature, as Speed (1984) and others (i.e. Hayley, 1971) have strongly indicated. It is nothing less than a radical shift of conceptualization in helping. People are seen to behave as a consequence of their interaction with others; communications between people thus become central to the concerns of the helper; the role of the person in creating their own distress experience is mediated by their interaction with others; the quality of interpersonal support becomes a central question for the helper to examine. Some workers, such as Walrond-Skinner (1981), suggest that family therapy techniques can be applied to individual therapy and individual therapy techniques can be applied to family therapy work – therefore these interventions have similar status in terms of the kinds of assumptions that are involved. The family focused form of helping involves a different orientation and set of assumptions about the origins and nature of distress experiences than those normally used when the individual is regarded as the focus for helping. Whilst the orientation differs – it sees the individual as a product of family processes – it is clearly the case that a variety of techniques (whatever their origination) can be used to help those in the family who seek the support of the helper.

This shift in orientation is radical, as can be seen in the way in which family focused helpers speak about the needs of the persons they are helping. Rather than speaking about these needs in terms of individuals (i.e. 'Jack's a very depressed person' or 'Mary has an awful lot of anger to get rid of' or 'Mike is confused'), the family focused helper is led to speak about 'the family's depression as currently shown by Jack' or 'the communication patterns which Mary has learned to use in the family and which she now finds generate angry behaviour' or 'the confusion Mike and others share'. This recognition of the interaction source of a person's behaviour leads to needs being conceived and described differently.

The shift is also clearly seen in some of the kinds of interventions and techniques which family focused helpers sometimes use in their work. For these interventions are not simply designed to alleviate the distress a particular person experiences, but also to affect the family such that the interpersonal sources of this distress are removed, changed or exposed. Such interventions are intended to reduce the levels of distress which exist between family members and within the person who initially presents their distress. Whilst the techniques are often identical to those used in individualized forms of helping, the motives for the use are very different, as we shall see. In our view, family focused helping differs from individualized helping primarily in orientation rather than in technique.

Family focused helping can take place in a variety of ways. Much of this book is devoted to descriptions and interpretations of different methods of family focused helping. In particular, we examine behavioural approaches, the approach to the family as a rule system and as a communication system, together with psychoanalytic approaches to family focused work. Some of the more recent applications of these techniques to work with families will also be examined. Case material derived from the authors' own experiences and those of others will be used to illuminate some of the practices which these forms of helping involve.

It needs to be said clearly here that family focused helping does not require that the helper work with an entire family. Mother, father and children do not have to be present in order that family focused helping can take place. Family focused helping is a way of thinking about the nature of distress, the construction of need which a person expresses when seeking help and a way of structuring some helping activity; it is not, therefore, synonymous with the number of persons involved in the helping relationship (Wynne, 1971). The issue for the helper is not whether to see the family as a whole or an individual member of that family (though this is often a relevant question), but whether he or she regards the task in terms of affecting the family's interactions in some way. Murray Bowen (a leading American therapist), for example, has argued that he is often working in a family focused way with an individual because he is seeking to encourage that individual to affect patterns of interaction with other family members if they can be seen to be perpetuating his or her distress. It is equally possible to envisage a helper working in an individualized way with the family present. The number of persons in the room with a helper at any one time is *not* a statement of the nature of the helping that is taking place, at least in the terms of the distinctions so far made here.

The same argument applies to another form of helping, known as family network therapy (Speck and Rueveni, 1969). In this form of helping, all of those persons – family, neighbours, friends, teachers, doctors, relatives, social workers, workmates, clergy, and others – who play a significant role in a distressed person's life are involved in the helping process. As many as 40 persons can be involved (Speck and Attneave, 1971). The purpose of working with such a large group is to affect the way in which members of a particular family interact so as to enhance the quality of the family's life, such that the extent and nature of individual and collective distress within the family is reduced. Though many others are present, the helping focus is clearly upon the family's interaction and rule-patterns. Family focused helping is therefore taking place, even in the midst of 40 or so other persons.

Much of the available literature examines family focused helping in terms of the skilled intervention of trained family therapists and family therapy-oriented social workers. But there is a growing interest in the insights and skills of family focused work amongst other helpers. For example, there is a stream of the literature which looks at the application of family focused ideas to the work of nurses (Mereness, 1968; Anderson, 1969) and another stream relating relevant constructs and skills to the work of clinical psychologists (Seeger, 1976; Clement, 1977). Barker (1980) has also done much to translate the work of the family therapists into a medical context. Our intention here is to provide further connections for counsellors, social workers, probation workers, educational and clinical psychologists and others who seek to offer helping services.

One final point here: though family focused helping has a long history, dating from the mid 1950s, it is still not widely accepted as being a distinctive and alternative form of constructing need and defining helper intervention. The current edition of the *Comprehensive Textbook of Psychiatry* (Kaplan *et al.*, 1980) devotes only eight of its 3365 pages to family therapy, giving most emphasis to individualized forms of helping, especially those derived from psychoanalysis. None the less, family therapy has a history, strong traditions and a voluminous literature (including several journals). It is not only a major territory for helping activity, but also a distinctive set of theories about the nature, origins and course of distress.

Individual, Family and Community

This chapter has made explicit the distinction between individually focused and family focused helping. Emphasis has been given not only to the implications of this distinction for the practice of helping but also for understanding the origins of distress – two features which will be explored fully throughout this text.

But this distinction is itself an oversimplification. First, families as units are affected by the ways in which the surrounding community evaluates their actions, shapes their environment and creates expectations and norms which are themselves distressing. For example, Hilary Graham (1980) offers an account of the anger and aggression mothers sometimes display towards their babies. She concludes that incidences of physical aggression towards children are in part due to family and individual features and in part due to the way in which models of contemporary motherhood put pressure on families to cope. That is to say, the idea within the community that a mother should be able to cope with the demands of a persistently crying child, however tired she feels, and that the seeking of professional or other help is a sign of weakness is as much a determinant of her behaviour as the mother's own personality and competences. A community pressure from an undefined source is a risk factor.

As a further illustration, consider the experience of discovering the signs of breast cancer. There is some evidence (see Lazarus and Launier, 1982) that the social stigma of being a cancer 'victim' (the terminology is interesting here) deters women from seeking medical confirmation and treatment at the first sign of symptoms. Thus, a social concern about status in the community affects the individual's behaviour in help-seeking when faced with a physical symptom of illness.

The examples of child abuse and cancer symptoms given here show that there is an interaction between need on the one hand and the person and his or her social environment on the other. Need can be examined in these cases (and many others) at the level of the person, the family and the community in which they live. The experience of distress can be located in terms of the way in which these three levels of experience – self, family, community – interact. Helping can thus be seen in terms of the focus for deciding upon the level and nature of intervention – the person, the family and/or the community.

Two examples of how helping can be community focused or multifocused will make the point about the choice of intervention level more strikingly.

The first concerns bereavement. When a person experiences the loss of a marriage partner he or she experiences a grieving process (see Murgatroyd and Woolfe, 1982, for a description of this process in detail). The helper working with the bereaved person can do so through one to one counselling aimed at helping that person to understand this grieving process and promoting the completion of the grief-work that it involves. Alternatively, a helper can work with the remaining family in order to develop new sets of relationships made more difficult by the loss of one member of the 'family system'. A third course is open to a helper: he or she may choose to connect this person to others who have been through or are going through similar experiences. In fact there is a particular organization (known as CRUSE) which exists precisely for this reason. Such a connection with others enhances the network of personal contacts with relevant experiences for the bereaved person whilst at the same time providing a network of social support. This last strategy we term here a community focus. Many helpers will use one or more of these levels when helping the bereaved person. Our point here is that the choice of focus for helping needs to be explicit and conscious.

A second example of a community focus concerns rape. The victim of rape can experience a great many emotional, social and physical reactions which require the help of another person. This helper may choose to work with the person as an individual or may choose to work with the person's family as the focus for helping. In addition, the helper may seek to connect this person to a women's group or to a rape crisis centre. The connections made may serve different purposes: a connection to a women's group may be seen as promoting social support whilst enabling some consciousness raising work to take place; connection to a rape crisis centre may give rise to a specific campaign to change the practices of doctors, police, the law or social workers associated with the particular case. Rape is a personal and a social experience and can be worked through at these levels.

Distress

In choosing a level for intervention the helper will be guided by his or her own experience and by the nature of the distress displayed by the person in need. We therefore need to be clear about the meaning of the term distress.

Interestingly, the *Shorter Oxford English Dictionary* definition of distress embodies the points just made about levels of intervention. For it defines distress as 'anguish or affliction affecting the body, spirit or community' – implying that the alleviation of distress would involve the question of whether it arises in the body, the spirit or the community.

It is possible to envisage distress within a family as something which affects sections of our communities: unemployment and social deprivation being examples. Here we can suggest that the distress is a function of social and economic policies and the structure of our society. The distress that arises from these sources may be experienced differently by different families. But the origins of the distress are clearly located in the social system. Another conception of distress sees its origins in the emotional discomforts which a particular person experiences at a particular time. For example, distress appearing in the form of depression may result from the failure of the person to master a particular skill. Finally, distress may arise out of the tension felt between people who live or work in close proximity to each other – interpersonal distress. This distress may show itself in families in a variety of ways (i.e. bedwetting by a child, temper tantrums by an adolescent member of the family or violence between parents), but its origins can be traced to the quality of the interpersonal relationships between family members.

In this text we do not pretend to examine systematically the ways in which helpers could intervene at the level of social policy. However, it is important to note that these three forms of distress are not independent of each other. A helper who defines the distress of his or her 'clients' as essentially personal when those clients are experiencing unemployment is privvy to a great deal of insight which can be valuable if communicated to those campaigning for changes in social policies towards unemployed people. Such interactions between the levels of distress and intervention as briefly outlined here constitute important areas for helpers to be aware of. It reinforces the point made earlier that helpers need to make conscious choices about their levels of intervention and to do so on the basis of careful assessment of both the nature and origins of distress.

The Helper's Decision

The preceding sections have made clear that the helper, when faced with a person in distress, has to make a conscious choice concerning the way in which he or she is to define distress and a choice as to the appropriate level of intervention for this person. In essence, three questions have to be answered. These are as follows: (a) What is the nature of this person's distress? (b) What are the origins of this experience? (c) What level do I want to intervene at?

These questions are very broad. From a practical point of view they are too broad. The following is a breakdown into more specific questions which the helper needs to address early in his or her contact with the person in need:

What is the nature of this person's distress?
   What behaviour indicates this distress?
   What thinking processes are at work in maintaining this distress?
   What emotional experiences typify this distress?
   What images does the person have when considering his or her distress?
   Who else is involved in maintaining this distress?
   What coping behaviours is the person using?
   What do they say causes their distress?
   How severe does the distress appear to be?
   How like any previous distress is this experience for this person?

What are the origins of this experience?
   To what extent is this distress due to this person or others?
   Is this person a symptom of the needs of others?
   Who else perpetuates the distress experience of the person – are they family members or unspecified others?
   What is the nature of this person's coping behaviour?
   What consequences does this person's coping behaviour have for his or her experience of distress?
   To what extent can this person's distress be regarded as a consequence of the situation – how typical is it?
   What are the atypical features of the distress – what do these features tell us about this person?
   What is the context (individual, family, other) in which the experience of distress has developed?

What level do I want to intervene at?
   Will working at the level of this person's own experience change the level of distress?
   Will I have to work on the part this person plays in his or her family in order to affect the experience of distress?
   What effect would working in this way have upon other family members – who in the family might now become distressed?
   Is this person able to act as an 'agent' for change within the family?
   Can I cope with the 'others' who might be involved here – what is comfortable for me as a helper?

Can I work at more than one level here – the individual, the family and/or the community?
What are the potentials of this person's situation for community development?
What skills do I have that are appropriate – who else can I involve?
How will I know if change has occurred and if this change is 'productive'?

This list seeks to make several points. First, there is a need for the helper to understand fully the distress being presented by the person in need. This involves exploring the way the person thinks, feels and behaves, the roles of others in promoting and maintaining the distress, its urgency and severity and the way in which the person in need is attempting to cope with the experience of distress. Only a careful assessment of its nature is likely to lead to appropriate helping action.

Next, understanding the nature of distress is not enough of a guide to the helper who sees him- or herself as having choice over the level and focus of intervention. The helper also needs to know more about the origins of this distress. This involves the helper in the attempt to disentangle the various influences of family and friends, personality and social and economic factors. Whilst some of the questions to be asked in relation to this second topic area – the origins of the distressing experience – overlap with the first area, the intention in asking these questions is different. The helper has moved from 'What is this distress?' to 'Where does this distress come from?' as the core question.

Finally, the helper needs, on the basis of his or her understanding of the distress and its origins, to decide on the appropriate level of intervention. This decision – crucial to all subsequent helping activity – involves questions about both the appropriateness of a helping strategy to the person's needs and about the competences of the helper. In addition, the making of a conscious choice about how to help a person in need also begs questions about how this help is to be evaluated.

It is not our intention in providing this list that helpers should quiz those who seek their help by asking the questions presented. Rather, the list is intended to sharpen the helpers' thinking about the conscious decisions they will need to make. The list is also intended to make clear that there are choices between definitions of distress (personal, interpersonal and social) and levels of intervention (person, family, community).

Conclusion

This chapter has examined the way in which helpers define their role when faced with a person in distress. Whilst there is a sense in which distress is always an intensely personal experience, distress is seen as having varied roots which need to be understood if helping is to be effective. Furthermore, helpers need to make conscious choices about helping strategies if their helping is to be more than a 'suck it and see' approach for those in need of their services. Work at the level of the individual as 'client', family relationships as 'client' or the community as 'client' are all forms of helping that can be considered as aiming to alleviate distress. With some persons experiencing distress all three forms of helping may be needed; with others only one will be appropriate. The choice is critical to the success of the helper.

In considering these points we have given emphasis to individual and family focused helping, since these are within our competence and provide the focus for this text. We wish here to reiterate the importance of community development and community action, as well as the work of support, pressure and special interest groups in providing a focus for helping. Whilst we are not able here fully to describe and to elaborate on the work of such groups, it is important to recognize that they do constitute a significant framework for personal, family and community development. From time to time we will return to their roles, but they are not the object of the materials in this text. Instead we focus upon the ways in which helpers can work with individuals and families so as to alleviate distress.

2
HOW DO FAMILIES CREATE DISTRESS?

Introduction

Distress is a subjective not an objective phenomenon. While people (families) share similar life events, they experience these events in different ways. Thus, while the occurrence may, on the face of it, be the same, the meaning of the experience differs from family to family. The purpose of this chapter is to set these experiences in a social and cultural perspective, which takes account of some key characteristics of our contemporary society, like high unemployment and the changing role of women. It is in such a context that the cycle of family life is shaped and develops. Through this exercise, we can explore the extent to which family life contains the potential for distress, conflict and crisis. While the potential for distress may be seen as residing in many areas of life faced by families, how it is dealt with and whether or not it becomes a source of stress are functions of the family's coping or adaptational mechanisms. Thus coping is an important concept in this discussion and indeed is to be seen not just as a reaction to a circumstance, but as a shaper of that event.

Equilibrium and the Family

In our culture, the family occupies a central role. For most people, the idea of life without some sort of family structure to provide a source of caring, comfort and emotional security is unthinkable. We tend to treat the role of the family and the value of what it does for the individual as some sort of self-evident, obvious truth. Terms like socialization, financial support during periods of dependence, and sexual and emotional fulfilment roll off the tongue in thinking about the functions of the family and are to be found in hundreds of textbooks on the subject. These accounts see the family as having a function within society; that is to say, families can have positive consequences in the sense of helping to maintain social and economic stability and equilbrium. In this model, which is sometimes described by sociologists as structural–functional, the world is seen as a system consisting of interconnected parts, the idea of system being crucial. These parts are in a state of equilibrium, so that if one part of the system changes, changes take place elsewhere, restoring the totality to its original state of 'balance' or equilibrium. If these ideas are difficult to grasp, we can think of them as applied to the human body (a system). If one part of that system (e.g. a finger) becomes infected, changes happen elsewhere (e.g. antibodies are developed) which seek to restore the system to its original state.

This approach can be seen in a number of important books on family therapy. In a pioneering textbook, Satir (1967) points out that 'numerous studies have shown that the family behaves as if it were a unit'. She adds that in 1954, Jackson introduced the term 'family homeostasis' to refer to this behaviour (see Jackson, 1957). By this he means the following: (a) that the family acts so as to achieve a balance in its relationships; (b) that members help to maintain this balance both overtly and covertly; (c) that the family's repetitious, circular, predictable communication patterns reveal this balance; (d) that when the equilibrium appears precarious, family members exert much effort to maintain it.

Minuchin (1974) also uses the terms 'system' and 'function' in describing the family. He talks about family structure as 'the invisible set of functional demands that organizes the ways in which family members interact' and a family is 'a system that operates through transactional patterns'. He adds that 'the system maintains itself. It offers resistance to change beyond a certain range and maintains preferred patterns as long as possible. Alternative patterns are available within the system. But any deviation that goes beyond the system's threshold of tolerance elicits mechanisms which re-establish the accustomed range.'

Conflict and the Family

While the perception of the family as a system has been an important and radical one in therapy in focusing attention away from individual pathology and on to family relationships, its emphasis on equilibrium has a number of wider implications of which it is helpful to be aware.

In particular, the stress on 'system maintenance' tends to obscure the fact that the interests of different parts of the system (such as different members of the family) may not coincide or that equilibrium may be obtained by one party imposing its power on another. The more we acknowledge the importance of conflict, the more important becomes the notion of power. For instance men on the whole have greater economic power than women and adults tend to have power over children. While structural family therapy may recognize the idea of power implicitly, a more overtly sociological analysis would point explicitly to power as a chronic characteristic of social systems and that in the context of the family the relationship between men and women hardly begins as one based on equality. To acknowledge this fact is to acknowledge the manner in which relationships within the family are located within culturally and socially defined parameters.

Once we begin to look at the family in this way (or for that matter, any institution in society), then we expose ourselves to models of the family other than those with which we have been brought up and which we find comfortable. For example, we may be forced to acknowledge a basic conflict of interest between social classes, racial or religious groups (at the macro societal level) and between men and women or adults and children (at the micro level of the family).

When applied specifically to the family, this type of conflict theory has led to a number of critiques about the role of the family in contemporary society and the following three sets of arguments stand out with particular force:

The Family is an Obstacle to the Liberation of Women

The argument runs that the traditional economic arrangements of the man as the wage earner and the woman as the person responsible for household domestic arrangements have produced an unequal relationship between men and women. By being economically dependent on their husbands, women have become subservient to men. This process has been reinforced first by the myth of 'motherhood' which defines this division as normal and secondly by increasing male control over women's capacity to reproduce. Domestication, therefore, places women in a subordinate position to men and critically influences their roles, experiences and identity. Thus, while the family may indeed have a function within society (i.e. it helps society to maintain and perpetuate itself), it performs this function at the expense of women. Furthermore, the sexual division of labour within the family ensures that, when in paid employment, women represent a more flexible workforce than men. They are less likely to be unionized, to be in well paid jobs, or to register as unemployed. Under the second Thatcher government there has been a call for women to move away from the world of work back into the home in order to care for the sick, handicapped and elderly. Women are, therefore, being specifically requested to express a supportive and nurturing role. By doing so they reduce further their own economic power both by accepting the burden of meeting the needs created by reduced state provision for the needy and by increasing the number of jobs available to men.

Inevitably such a brief account simplifies complex arguments and blurs the boundaries between complex ideas: between, for example, patriarchal and Marxist explanations of sexual divisions. The latter school of thought argues that the location of women's primary role in the spheres of reproduction and domestication only arose with the development of capitalism. This produced a privatized family by stripping away the links between childbearing and economic production. At another level, Marxist explanations argue that the notion of women as a sisterhood, oppressed by men, obscures the different manner in which different classes of women experience the sexual division of labour. For example, so far as living style and standards are concerned, the middle-class woman has more in common with middle-class males than she has with her working-class female counterparts, or so the argument runs.

However, our purpose in this book is not to explore in detail the variety of perspectives available to explain this sexual division of labour, but rather to indicate the way in which all these perspectives illuminate for us a view of the family and its functions which is quite different to conventional notions of the family as a self-evidently beneficial and worthwhile institution (see the work of Greer, 1970; Millet, 1970; Oakley, 1976). What such critiques say is essentially that families are better for some than for others.

The Family is Essentially Privatizing and Antisocial

There are a number of strands to this line of reasoning which, though they derive from different angles, nevertheless go together to make up a coherent statement. One strand, already alluded to, is historical and points to the rise of capitalism (or others would point to the factory system or industrialization or technological change) as the vehicle which broke up traditional family structures which often extended across a number of generations. The move from country to town and from agriculture to industry involved the separation of home and work as well as the break-up of the extended family. It produced what we now know as the nuclear family. A more modern variant of this line of reasoning points to the post-war reconstruction of urban Britain, which involved the break-up of closely linked and integrated working-class communities, with a concomitant development of suburbs and new towns (see Young and Willmott, 1957; Willmott and Young, 1960). These new communities lacked such a clear sense of their identity. As a result, the nuclear family is not just cut off from its wider kinship network but has only tenuous links in the community in which it exists. Social and geographical mobility may be seen as exacerbating this tendency.

A second strand of this argument derives from the experience of centrally organized societies seeking to bring about rapid social change. China is a good example. Such countries have been forced to acknowledge the power of the family to frustrate change by perpetuating old values concerning religion, the sexual division of labour, the socialization of children, social classes, etc. Accordingly social engineering has been concerned to open up the family for exposure to a wider set of communal values. However, this form of social engineering should not be seen as simply a product of centralized societies. The Israeli *kibbutz* movement (see Bettelheim, 1968) represents a similar attempt to ensure, by breaking down traditional family structures, that the values of the society are clearly and uniquivocally communicated across generations and that change is not undermined from within by the covert withdrawal of consent. Minuchin (1974) points out that

> 'attacks on the family are typical of revolutionary periods. Christ told his disciples to leave their parents and families and to follow him. The French, Russian and Chinese revolutions all undermined the traditional family structure in those countries in an attempt to speed the progress towards a new social order. The Israeli Kibbutz is another example of the same social process' (Minuchin, 1974).

In contemporary Britain we have taken a somewhat different approach to social engineering and on the whole have tended to try to bolster and support the family. A return to so-called Victorian family values, however mythical, now appears as a standard rallying call. It is significant that contemporary explanations of social pathologies like delinquency, vandalism and violence frequently point to a decline in family values and solidarity as a prime causal factor. While on the whole we try to support and reform rather than to restructure (in other words our remedy differs), our diagnosis of the state of the family may not be all that different from societies with which, on the face of it, we have little in common. The common analysis is that the family, by being a 'privatized unit', has the power to resist or at best fail adequately to support societal objectives and values.

The Family is a Container in which Individuals are Manipulated and Exploited

This line of argument flows logically from the idea of the family as a system whose parts (individual members) may be in a state of harmony or conflict. In looking at families in distress, it is clearly the conflict situation in which we are interested. While this may seem a fairly obvious proposition, it is not one which has always been recognized in the history of therapy. Traditionally, attention has focused on the parts rather than the whole; on the trees rather than the wood. Psychodynamic theories of personality have long been concerned with unresolved conflicts within the individual: the idea of the family as a unit in conflict is a relatively new one. Why should this be so? Perhaps the answer lies in the ideological importance of the family in our society as an agent of cultural reproduction? This creates a powerful resistance to the idea that what happens within the family may be pathological for some of its individual members. Put another way, we can say that it is ideologically threatening, and therefore difficult, to suggest that equilibrium (the *status quo*) may have negative as well as positive features. Translated into the language of mental health, we are saying that equilibrium may be created around a situation in which some individuals are able to impose and satisfy their emotional needs upon and at the expense of others. The work of Laing (see Laing and Esterson, 1970; Laing, 1971; Cooper, 1971) is radical not just because it challenges conventional psychiatric notions of mental illness, but because it threatens the basis of two central ideological buttresses of our society, namely that equilibrium is intrinsically healthy and that the family unit is essentially a sound model through which the process of becoming a socialized person can be experienced.

Some Empirical Facts

We have indicated that while these critiques derive from a variety of disciplines, including sociology, history and psychiatry, they have a lowest common denominator, in that their theoretical bases perceive the world as a phenomenon in which conflict is a major component part. Now, of course, theories do not derive *in vacuo*, but are rooted in the societies from which they derive. It is instructive, therefore, to look at a number of empirical phenomena which have given support and impetus to our perception of society as chronically characterized by conflict. These include: (a) the development of a youth culture, which on the face of it appears to find traditional values incorporated within the family, repressive and inhibiting; (b) growing evidence about the incidence of physical violence within the family – this includes one partner (usually the man) against the other, adults against children, and sometimes parents against grandparents; (c) the increase in the percentage of couples getting divorced, followed by an even higher percentage among couples getting married for the second time; (d) the greater number of couples prepared to cohabit without getting married – this has led to a whole new language to describe such relationships, e.g. 'live-in partner', 'cohabitee', etc.; (e) the growth in unemployment, which has damaged the traditional view of the man as wage earner supporting an economically dependent wife and children.

It is not our intention to describe each of these phenomena in detail and anyway the list itself is not exhaustive. However, a few facts offer a useful illustrative aid as an indicator of the extent to which family structure can be regarded as being in a state of flux, and a critical criterion is surely divorce. Table 1 (extracted from *Social Trends 1984*, Table 2.14: Central Statistical

Table 1   The numbers and proportions of divorce, 1961–1982

Year	Divorces granted (UK)	Divorces per 1000 married couples (England and Wales)
1961	27 000	2.1
1971	80 000	6.0
1976	136 000	10.1
1977	138 000	10.4
1978	153 000	11.6
1979	148 000	11.2
1980	160 000	12.0
1981	157 000	11.9
1982	159 000	12.0

Office, 1984) indicates the general rise in the numbers of divorces granted between 1961 and 1982. As the data shows, the divorce rate doubled between

1971 and 1982, though the Divorce Law Reform Act of 1971 (of which we shall say more in a moment) was a factor here. Age at marriage is a strong correlate of the likelihood of divorce. To take 1982 as an example, of all divorces granted in that year (in Great Britain) 37.3 percent involved couples where the wife had been less than 20 years old at marriage and another 42.8 percent involved couples where the wife had been between 20 and 24 years of age (*Social Trends 1984*, Table 2.15: Central Statistical Office, 1984). The official commentary on the table remarks that 'if 1980–1981 divorce rates were to persist unchanged, it is estimated that almost three in five teenage bachelor grooms and one in two teenage spinster brides would eventually divorce'.

As we have already pointed out, these changes were partly a function of the Divorce Law Reform Act of 1971 which changed the grounds upon which divorce could be obtained in England and Wales, so that the sole grounds for divorce became evidence of the 'irretrievable breakdown of marriage'. Divorce could be obtained after two years of separation upon the agreement of both parties and after five years' separation upon the decision of one party. While legal changes may have precipitated this increase, the fact that it took place at all is an indication of how many marriages in distress must have existed before the passing of the Act. Not that marriage itself is any less popular as an institution. The commentary in *Social Trends 1984* (Central Statistical Office, 1984, p. 36) suggests that 'of women who separated between 1970 and 1974 before the age of 35, nearly a quarter (23%) had remarried within three years, while just over half (52%) had remarried within six years'. This is in part an expression of the lack of institutional and emotional support for the state of singleness in our society, but it would also seem to say something about the expectations which people now hold about marriage. The traditional notion of man as the bread winner and woman as the housewife has given way to a more profound set of expectations. In the words of a consultative document by a government working party on marriage guidance

> 'the trend which can be identified is that marriage is increasingly required to serve the partners' own personal development, thereby throwing into relief the level of their capacity for close and intimate personal relationships . . . our evidence and experience confirm the thesis that personal development and satisfaction are core values underlying contemporary expectations of marriage' (Home Office, 1979, p. 21).

Given such expectations it is not perhaps surprising that in many second marriages there is to be found a rate of divorce even higher than for first marriages. Almost one in five divorces (18.5 percent) in England and Wales in 1982 involved at least one partner who had already been divorced, compared with almost one in 10 (8.8 percent) in 1971 and 9.3 percent in 1961 (*Social Trends 1984*, Table 2.14: Central Statistical Office, 1984). As the table commentary puts it,

> 'on the assumption that divorce rates remain at the 1980–1981 levels . . . the chance that the marriage of a divorced man would again end in divorce is one and a half times higher than that of a single man who marries at the same age. Similarly, a divorced woman who remarries is approximately twice as likely to divorce as a single woman who marries at the same age' (Social Trends, 1984, p. 36).

Without going too deeply into the reasons for this phenomenon, a number of pertinent comments are made in the following passage from an article in *The Guardian* (Faulder, 1984):

> 'Renate Olins, Director of the London Marriage Guidance Council, believes that too often a second marriage is called upon to heal the wounds of the first. "Women particularly" she says, "are often lured by the destructive challenge – she didn't understand him but I do" . . . . there are other hazards, too, like the luggage of bitterness and financial burdens which people bring with them into a second marriage. A woman who marries a man with a family is taking on a man who is mortgaged to his past. And a woman who has been married before can't deny her sexual experience, something which men especially seem to find hard to take. Then there's jealousy, a very potent factor, which can turn the most innocent comment into dynamite.'

The article continues, 'in a second marriage expectations are heightened but the tolerance threshold is lowered. The memory of what was good about the first marriage can fatally vitiate the second, because irrationally people would like every marriage to be like the ideal first one they never had' (Faulder, 1984).

A final comment about this data refers to its inevitable effect upon children and the growth in the number of one-parent families. The Finer Report of 1974 estimated that there were 620 000 one-parent families, of which 60 percent were caused by separation or divorce. In 1981, 60 percent of couples divorcing had children under the age of 16 (*Social Trends 1984*, Table 2.16: Central Statistical Office, 1984). As a result of the divorces in this one year alone, 169 000 children aged under 16 became members of single-parent families: of these children, two-thirds were aged under 11, and a quarter were under five years old (*Social Trends 1984*, Table 2.16).

Increasingly, therefore, it is becoming less and less appropriate to define the typical family as comprising a man, a woman and their offspring. In 1961, the percentage of lone parents with dependent children represented 2 percent of all households. By 1982, this had risen to 4 percent (*Social Trends 1984*, Table 2.4) and the trend seems to be upwards. Perhaps not unrelated is the fact that in 1982 there were 93 200 children in the care of local authorities (DHSS, 1984), though this figure is falling as fostering increases at the expense of care in residential institutions.

The Life-cycle of the Family

The present period of high unemployment has also produced significant changes in family structure. In an increasing percentage of families, it is now the woman who is the chief wage earner. The growth in youth unemployment has also had consequences in blurring the traditional passage by which a child leaves school, gets a job and finally leaves home. While this account of change is highlighting external events as imposing an imperative for change upon families, it would be misleading to perceive the relationship between such events and the internal dynamics of the family in a purely mechanistic way. The relationship is complex, as we shall indicate in ensuing chapters. Moreover, despite this state of flux and change, the traditional family developmental cycle remains a powerful structure in which the hopes and expectations of individuals are shaped and expressed. Life is not static, rather it's a moveable feast. Individuals are born, grow-up, get married, have children of their own and finally die. Families provide a structure through which these events take place and are thus, by the very nature of normal growth and development, subject to the vagaries of vicissitude and change. Individuals go through the processes first of identification with parents and then of independence and separation. Parents have to adjust to the challenge of new family members when a child is born and losing these members when the child finally grows up and becomes independent and ultimately leaves home. It is hardly surprising, therefore, that the literature is full of discussion of the various crises faced by young families as they cope with coming to terms with their own fantasies through their marital relationship, coping with children, adolescence, these children leaving home, old age and so on. In a well known work, Sheehy (1977) refers to these as 'predictable' crises of adult life. However, we should not take this description too literally. It implies that we all experience the same set of events at roughly the same time as a crisis. These assumptions should be challenged. Nicholson (1980, p. 21), for example, argues that 'when we do change in adulthood, it is not as a result simply of the passage of time, but rather because of major life-events, many (though not all) of which we wish upon ourselves'. Major events like marriage, divorce, illness or unemployment can change people, but this may happen whatever the age period at which the event happens. We should also beware of accepting too readily that these events are necessarily to be regarded as crises. For some families this may well be the case, but for others the natural passage of events is experienced without obvious signs of trauma or distress. It would be nice to be able to explain simply why this is so, but while prescriptions may be impossible, some elementary (but none the less valuable) guidelines can be indicated.

The Normal and the Pathological

All families develop patterns concerned with the allocation of roles and the attribution of authority. These derive in part from the expectations of the wider society internalized in individual men and women. However, they also take account of the psychological needs of individual people, often experienced unconsciously rather than consciously, and relating to concerns such as authority, submission, dominance, control and power. The family is not just an arena in which children are brought up, it is also an arena in which two adults seek to satisfy their own needs and live out and resolve their own conflicts and fantasies. In introducing their book *Families, and How to Survive Them* (Skynner and Cleese, 1983), the authors remark that it is 'about normal, everyday families: it's the everyday story of paranoia, repression, role-reversals, manic behaviour, jealousy between husbands and wives, and between parents and children' (see also Skynner et al., 1983). In other words, the line between normal and pathological is really a very fine one. This is an important point. It is tempting to see normality as a state in which there is an absence of pain, fear, anxiety, anger or other negative feelings, but this is a very misleading picture. Reluctance to express negative feelings is itself an indicator of lack of self-confidence exemplified by such beliefs that if I express my anger or annoyance or irritation, the object of my feelings will stop loving me or will not like me anymore or will be nasty to me. The result is often frustration and lack of self-assertiveness. Moreover, fear and anger and anxiety are themselves raisers of adrenaline and motivators. As students awaiting an examination or athletes contemplating a sporting event readily appreciate, feeling too self-confident or relaxed is an actual barrier to peak performance. In other words, low and moderate levels of anxiety, which the person can recognize and manage, have a positive 'turn-on' capacity. More generally, the perception of emotional health and illness as a black and white division flows from a view of life as a product rather than as a process. The inherent dangers of such a perception are brilliantly illustrated in Laing's well known lines (Laing, 1970):

> 'He does not think there is anything the matter with him because
> one of the things that is
> the matter with him
> is that he does not think that there is anything
> the matter with him
> therefore
> we have to help him realize that,
> the fact that he does not think there is anything
> the matter with him
> is one of the things that is
> the matter with him.'

Normality, therefore, is not the achievement of a state of perfection, but is represented by the acceptance that negative feelings are 'okay' provided that they are acknowledged and expressed in a sensitive manner, that fantasies (conscious) and phantasies (unconscious) are a characteristic of all people, that the human being is a mixture of adult and child, and that we all have parts of ourselves that we would like to adapt and change. The idea of 'working at a relationship' involves two or more people openly exploring their problems together, fully aware of how one affects and is affected by the other.

Against this background it is hardly surprising to find that the birth of a child is often experienced by one partner as the arrival of a rival, or that adolescent children create problems for parents as the young person's growing sexual expressions arouse fears and anxieties in parents about their own sexuality. Simultaneously a challenge may be offered to the authority of the parents. We can go on and on with this kind of example. The time when children leave home has implications in its withdrawal of the nurturing role and forces a reappraisal by both partners of their aims and objectives and general satisfaction with life. How families cope with these stresses is at least in part a function of their ability to be flexible, their awareness of the processes which are being experienced, their capacity to respond in a manner which is characterized by open communication, the expression of feelings (both negative and positive) and a level of maturity which recognizes the desirability of meeting the needs of all family members. Generally speaking, it involves a need to recognize and to deal with conflict as and when it arises.

Unemployment

These comments also apply to the stresses and strains of illness, handicap, divorce and unemployment, all of which involve some form of restructuring of role divisions established within the family. It is interesting to examine these effects in the context of work and unemployment, an increasingly important characteristic of contemporary society. As we have pointed out elsewhere (Murgatroyd and Woolfe, 1982) job loss can be characteristically and symbolically represented 'as a form of separation, with all the associated forms of attachment, loss and grief-work which has come, following Bowlby, to be associated with such separations'. A typical expression of grieving as a consequence of job loss can be discussed under an number of headings:

(a) *Loss* There is a sense of loss of activity and security – 'a part of me has disappeared', 'it's like losing a limb', 'my whole purpose in life has disappeared' are typical responses we have come across.
(b) *Searching* The feeling of loss soon merges into the task of searching, not just for another job, but at a deeper level for 'the real me' or 'to do what I would really like to do'.
(c) *Re-finding* The process of searching typically produces a period of action such as jobs around the house or domestic duties previously carried out by the spouse which appears to suggest that the person has found purposeful work. Other members of the family (their roles) may be affected by these events.
(d) *Re-loss* Eventually the re-found activities are found to contain a lack of purpose which leads to re-loss, a difficult stage in the process of grief as a result of job loss. Associated with this stage are a number of features which may have major consequences for the rest of the family. These include (i) denial of the consequences of being unemployed, frequently associated with alcoholism; (ii) withdrawal from the reality of the situation, leading to depression and illness; (iii) the development of learned helplessness; (iv) freezing of both affect and action; (v) hostility towards other family members, particularly towards those in work; (vi) the development

of feelings of guilt and atonement often demonstrated in obsessional behaviour unlikely to lead to a resolution of the underlying problem, namely lack of paid employment.

It is likely that the person will alternate to and fro between these stages until either a job is found or a more adaptive response to the situation is developed, with the help of members of the family or wider support network. This leads to two further stages:

(e) *Awareness* The person now more readily understands his (or her) situation and its effect on other family members and develops a frame of thinking and feeling which accompanies a more realistic assessment of the situation in which he (she) finds himself (herself).

(f) *Burial* The view of self present at the start of the grieving process is finally put to rest. The emotional catharsis of the previous stages means that the person is better able to cope with the situation and with the feelings involved.

This model is useful in looking not just at job loss but at the situation experienced by many young people of being unable to find a first job. In this case the grief is in relation to an ideal, which concerns the opportunity to enter paid work. But whether the person in question is a wage earner or a young person leaving school, it is important to note what we can describe as a 'ripple effect' upon the rest of the family. All members of the family are likely to be affected by it. It influences self-image, roles, relationships and social standing.

In many ways work is the dominating determinant of family roles. Traditionally, man is the provider, woman is the nurturer and supporter, children are dependent. There is a direct link between the sexual and age divisions of labour and the emotional repertoires which work makes available to individuals. Job loss by the male, therefore, serves to blur differences between generations and creates confusion over roles, and thereby identities, between man and woman, particularly if the latter becomes the main wage earner. Just as job loss by the father may be a significant source of distress within the family, so can the failure by adolescent members of the family to secure work. Work represents an important transitional event, a boundary marker in the life of the young person. It represents a step on the road to economic independence and emotional individuation. The choice of career may also be of significance as an indication of the sameness or difference from family models and expectations. The barring of this developmental avenue may thus have significant consequences for all members of the family. It may involve a significant process of reappraisal for parents and children if any event disturbs the expected pattern of events. Overall, the failure of a member of a family to meet the work expectation affects the family's interpretation of its status as a family within the community as well as the component individuals' perceptions of the person in question and the overall internal dynamics and relationships of that family.

Distress

Distress can take many forms. For example, scapegoating is a situation in which blame or guilt or shame is projected on to one member of the family, such that this person comes to be the repository of the family's inability to express and discharge painful feelings and unresolved conflict. In this adaptation, unresolved conflict may be more overtly expressed in verbal or even physical violence. Dobash and Dobash (1974) suggest that conflicting role expectations are more likely to lead to a situation which terminates in violence when the following four conditions are satisfied: (a) the issue is of great importance either to both parties or at least to the one for whom violence is a form of emotional expression; (b) the violation of expectations is blatant or extreme – an example might be a family's withdrawal of traditional male privileges from a man who had lost his job; (c) role expectations are so rigid and lacking in flexibility that even minor deviations are unacceptable, e.g. where job loss by the man takes place in a situation where the philosophies embodied in the sexual division of labour are absolutely fixed and unchangeable; (d) where expectations are so unrealistic that violations are almost inevitable – for example, the belief that job loss or failure to find work will have no effects whatsoever on family relationships.

Clearly scapegoating and physical violence represent just two examples of conflictual situations which are not resolved. But there are many others. Those who work in marriage guidance counselling will identify only too readily the many forms of marital disharmony engendered by lack of communication in which partners are not aware of the unconscious elements of self which are driving their behaviour.

Successful Coping

Of course, the opposite side of the coin to conflict is cohesion and this concept has been identified (Orford, 1980) as a key concept in the consideration of family stability and conversely distress. Orford defines the core characteristic of the cohesive family in terms of eight factors spelt out by Moos and Moos (1976). These are: (1) more time spent in shared activity; (2) less withdrawal, avoidance and segregated activity; (3) a high rate of warm interactions, and a lower rate of critical or hostile interactions amongst members; (4) fuller and more accurate communication between members; (5) a more favourable evaluation of other members and/or a lower level of criticism of other members; (6) more favourable meta-perceptions, i.e. members are more likely to assume that other members have a favourable view of them; (7) a higher level of perceived affection between members; (8) a higher level of satisfaction and morale, and greater optimism about the future stability of the family group.

Orford argues that families which lack these characteristics 'put their members at risk of experiencing psychological distress' and that 'particularly vulnerable will be those family members who are already at risk for other reasons'. Reciprocally, when social cohesion is high, families are more likely to cope with a variety of stress-inducing conditions. The cohesive family 'provides its members with information about the world, guides its members' behaviour, provides a set of values, helps problem-solve, provides practical aid and a place of sanctuary, validates members' self-identities, assists in emotional mastery and in general fosters a feeling of security and competence'. He concludes that family therapy of whatever form can basically be said to work 'if and when it brings about an increment in family cohesion'.

We can also point to the dimension of flexibility–rigidity as a crucial aspect in evaluating the family's ability to cope with potentially stressful events, so that they do not become distressing. But what do we mean by flexibility or for that matter rigidity? To say that any family which avoids distress is flexible, while another which experiences it is rigid, simply produces a tautology. There is no way in which the theory can be disproved. A major contributor to the field of coping mechanisms is Richard Lazarus, who has expressed his conviction that coping must be flexible to be effective. While Lazarus defines the term implicitly rather than explicitly, the major thrust behind the idea of flexibility is well expressed in the following quotation from his work (Lazarus, 1978):

> 'We conventionally treat a process of coping as a static state of mind rather than as a constant search for a way of comprehending what is happening, a way that seeks simultaneously to test reality and to retain hope. Depending on the moment, the circumstance, the evidence, the social pressures, the personality,

such a construction remains always in flux, now moving one way, now another. Only severely disturbed persons display well-consolidated defenses that constantly resist uprooting.'

Lazarus sees this way of looking at the problem as close to Frankl's notion of a continuous effort at meaning (Frankl, 1963) and the way Erikson (1959) views the struggle in ageing to achieve integrity rather than despair:

> 'One does not arrive fixedly at one or the other pole of thought, but is constantly in tension between the two . . . this idea of constant tension between the polarities, of constant struggles to construe what is happening in one's existence, represents a dramatically different view of coping than the more traditional emphasis on trait, style or achieved structure'.

In some recent work Folkman and Lazarus (1980) identified the following eight coping styles commonly used by individuals facing some threatening or stressful life-event: (a) problem-focused coping, e.g. not acting too hastily; (b) wishful thinking, e.g. daydreaming; (c) detachment, e.g. waiting to see what happens; (d) seeking social support, e.g. talking to others; (e) focusing on the positive, e.g. rediscovering what is important in life; (f) self-blame, e.g. apologize; (g) tension reduction, e.g. take a vacation; (h) keep to self, e.g. keep feelings to oneself.

Lazarus would see flexibility as residing in having the ability to draw on a number of these strategies and to employ a strategy as appropriate as well as to switch from one to another. Emotionally healthy people are able to balance logical problem-solving techniques (using the intellect) with getting in touch with their feelings plus seeking support from social networks. In extreme cases, where people fail to cope with a crisis, Lazarus finds that there is an emphasis upon emotional expression, while the more cognitive, rational problem-solving strategies tend to get neglected. While the categories are constructed with individuals in mind, they seem to provide a useful focus for also looking at family coping mechanisms. In reflecting on the list it is necessary to avoid making hasty judgements about some of the categories. For example, while the denial of painful feelings may have damaging intra- or interpersonal effects in the long run, in the short run it may be an invaluable way of coping with potentially overwhelming feelings involved in, say, discovering that one has a serious illness or that one's newly born child is handicapped in some way.

The value of Lazarus' work lies particularly in the way it directs us towards a perception of distress and coping as a function of the transaction between the individual and his or her environment. It is just such a philosophy that underpins this chapter. In examining how families create distress we have been concerned to link together the internal dynamics of family life (or how a family copes with its relationships) and the influences of external events such as redundancy or illness. Among these we may include the natural and inevitable changes that occur as a person passes through life such as ageing, marriage, birth and death. So whether we realize it or not, the experience of life itself creates the potential for conflict and distress. The extent to which this is realized and experienced as distress is a subjective feature of how a family copes with its transactions within itself and with the wider world. The relationship, however, between external events and internal family dynamics is complex, but is one which needs to be carefully considered if we are to understand how families create distress.

In these first two chapters, we have been concerned to provide a springboard for the remainder of the book. In the chapters which follow, we have sought to articulate the relevance of the family as a focus for helping as seen by a number of different schools of thought. However, as we have already indicated, our aim is not to provide a textbook of family therapy, but to indicate to the helper, professional or voluntary, full-time or part-time – indeed anyone who regards helping others as a part of their work (counsellor, samaritan, doctor, nurse, health visitor, teacher, social worker, etc.) – how he or she can be more effective in his or her work by considering individuals in the context of the families in which they exist.

3

RULES, ROLES AND BOUNDARIES – HELPING AND FAMILY COMMUNICATIONS

Introduction

Family distress, as we have seen, has a great many roots and sources. In this chapter we examine the nature of distress as it arises from the patterns of communication and interaction amongst family members. Our aim in doing so is to illuminate the processes within families which create distress and to indicate some strategies which helpers can use when they are seeking to reduce distress and increase family well-being. In taking this approach readers need to be aware that the observations made in the previous chapter are not being put to one side. It is clear that many of the patterns of communication and interaction to be examined in this chapter arise out of the social structure of which families are a part. In particular, the place of a woman (especially woman as mother) in a family communication pattern is strongly related to the place of the woman in society and the power relationships exercised through family structures by men. But, as we have said, our aim is to offer insights into family life and distress which can be of direct benefit to helpers. We therefore narrow our focus to the level of the family system, bearing in mind the fact that this system is reflecting contradictions, conflicts and tensions in society.

Much of the material in this chapter is derived from the work of Salvador Minuchin, Mara Pelazzoli and Paul Watzlawick – all of whom are experienced family therapists who have been influential in guiding the work of other family therapists throughout the world. Our aim is not, however, to document exhaustively their therapeutic systems and practices and to show the evidence for their effectiveness; rather, we offer a statement of the ideas which underlie their thinking and practice so as to help family helpers who are not trained specialists in their work with families.

There are three basic themes in this chapter. These are as follows: (a) the observation that communication within families takes place within implicitly agreed rules and that these implicit rules are often distressing to one or more family members; (b) the implicit communication rules within families create roles which individuals within the family ritually play, sometimes to the distress of others; and (c) roles and rules, in addition to being related to the communication patterns of family members, are also concerned with the nature of the differences between different generations of family members (grandparents, parents, children, children's children) and the roles played by different generations can be a source of distress. These points may sound very theoretical. In fact, they are very clear areas of concern to helpers which have direct practical implications for their work. We present these themes here in terms of some basic ideas, some case material to illuminate the points made and some suggestions for helping families whose distress relates to one or more of the ideas explored. Throughout the concern is to be as practical as possible.

A number of the ideas introduced in this chapter are important to the understanding of other chapters of this book. In particular the idea of *boundaries* introduced here is important to a number of later observations, especially those made concerning the role of helping (Chapter 7) and the nature of psychodynamics (Chapter 4). The construct 'flexibility' in response to change, introduced here in the context of a discussion on adaptability, is also relevant to later discussions of coping (Chapter 6) and to the idea of a repertoire of coping skills. Finally, the idea that implicit rules can affect behaviour, discussed here in the context of interpersonal communication, is taken up later in this book through an exploration of cognitive reframing (Chapter 5). Because this chapter carries these concepts which are valuable to later understanding, the chapter is significantly longer than several others of those included in this text. This should not, however, deter the reader: sometimes it takes space to outline interesting and illuminating ideas.

Rules and Protocols

Communication takes place in families at a variety of levels. For example, there are explicit messages (e.g. 'You should not . . .', 'I want you to . . .') which are communicated verbally; there are verbal messages which say one thing but mean another (e.g. 'You are free to behave in any way you want, we've always told you that you could' or 'I don't mind what you do as long as it doesn't upset me in any way'); there are communications in which the verbal message says one thing (e.g. 'Yes, I'm happy . . .') whilst the non-verbal message says another (e.g. '. . . really, I'm unhappy'); finally, there are silences which shout loudly to family members.

In looking at the communication patterns in families much more is revealed about the family's emotional life than is evident from the words and phrases used. For example, it is often the case that family communications are patterned in a particular way. In one family, whenever the elder son, Roy (aged 17), asks for something from another family member, his father always argues that he should not need to ask for things now that he is working, his mother always defends Roy and the younger son (aged 11) gets upset that the mother and father appear to row so frequently. This communications sequence happens between three and five times a week, since it is triggered by any request for practical assistance from the elder son. The 11-year-old's distress can be seen as a direct response to this pattern of communication.

Not all such communication patterns have negative consequences. In the Jones family, all evening meals are accompanied by a humorous account of the day's activities by the individuals within the family – each family member 'competes' to provide the most amusing account of their day. Whilst the outsider may find this tiresome, family members regard this as an important 'unwinding' activity for the family and for each individual at the end of a hard day's work.

The point to note about communications in families is that they form patterns: communication follows some sort of rule system. Here are some examples of the kind of 'rules' operated by families with whom we have worked: (a) Mum only speaks in Dad's presence when Mum is asked a question by another family member (e.g. Dad or one of the two children); (b) the youngest son never finishes a statement (e.g. about what is happening to him at school or at the youth club) because an older child always interrupts; (c) the father, in his attempts not to get angry at the oldest son, whose behaviour and dress he finds unacceptable, gets angry with the youngest daughter for the slightest reason, despite the fact that she is rarely disobedient and very concerned to obtain her father's approval. These illustrations show that the patterns of interaction in a family can be rule-bound in a way that is distressing to one or more family members.

In looking at such patterns of communication within families, particular communication patterns can be especially distressing. For example, there are three patterns which are regarded by many as creating high levels of distress. The first is the double-bind or 'Catch 22'. In this pattern the person receiving the communication (usually a child in the family) receives two conflicting messages at the same time; if they take action on either message they lose face or status in some way. Bateson (1956) offers this description of a classic double-bind:

> 'A young man was in hospital . . . and was visited by his mother. He was glad to see her and impulsively put his arm around her shoulders, whereupon she stiffened. He withdrew his arm and asked, "Don't you love me anymore?" He then blushed, and she said, "Dear, you must not be so easily embarrassed and afraid of your feelings." The patient was only able to stay with her a few minutes more . . .'

The mother's communication here presents the young man (her son) with conflicting sets of messages. Put simply, he now is encouraged to think that 'If I am to keep my tie to Mother I must show her that I love her, but if I show her that I love her then I will lose her'. The mother's communication was so incongruent that this is the inevitable message this young man discerns. Whatever action he takes, he loses. Another example can be derived from an old Jewish joke. A mother buys her son two ties, both of which are very much liked by the son; whenever he wears one his mother says 'Don't you like the other one I bought you . . . is there something the matter with it or don't you love me anymore?' – for this young man, no choice of tie is possible. This is the double-bind and can be seriously distressing to one or more family members if it persists over time and if it applies across a variety of family situations.

The second pattern that is often seen to create distress is the 'me first' pattern. Families, at one level, are a collection of individuals bound together by circumstances and blood-ties. Whilst there is a great deal of shared experience within a family – even if it is only at the level of sharing resources – there is also a great deal of individualized experience within family life that requires privacy, respect for the person and respect for personal needs. Sometimes there is a conflict between the collective and the personal within the family and this is reflected in the pattern of communication within the family. This conflict becomes acute when an attempt by one family member to secure personal space threatens others. For example, Sheelagh (aged 18) shares her bedroom with her younger sister, Joy (aged 13). In order to gain advantage over Joy and to help her own 'campaign' for more privacy, Sheelagh has started to 'tell tales' on Joy – about her smoking and her relationships with boys. In retaliation, Joy has invented some fantastic stories about Sheelagh's sexual behaviour which are upsetting the family. Sheelagh's aim of using her 'tales' to get Joy out of her room into the spare bedroom so that she will have privacy has backfired on the family as a whole in that the parents now do not trust either girl and have set them the task of spying on each other, thus necessitating Joy and Sheelagh sharing the same room. Sheelagh's 'me first' strategy here had both the opposite effect to that intended and reduced her standing within the family.

The third communication pattern that we examine briefly here is that of non-communication. Sometimes the attempts at interaction made by one family member are either systematically ignored (this *is* unusual) or systematically misunderstood. This occurs either because the person fails to communicate their thoughts, feelings, needs or wants adequately or the family systematically does not want to hear the communication(s) offered. For example, John (aged 16) feels he is discovering that he is homosexual. He tries to talk about this first with his mother and then with his father. Both parents reject any suggestion that he might be or could feel homosexual and refuse to talk about this subject. Whenever the subject is mentioned, the conversation subject is changed by one or other of the parents. Other conversations John initiates are listened to by his parents until the point at which his own sexual identity is raised in some way. Though the example provided here concerns sexuality, the use of what might be called 'un-hearing' is not restricted to sex: it can apply to questions about careers, death and dying, illness, money . . . a whole variety of topics that affect individual family members intensely. It is a common communication pattern and leads from the idea that if you ignore a difficult statement, eventually the 'problem' the statement alludes to will go away. In our example here, if John stops talking about his feelings of homosexuality within the family then the family can think that he no longer has homosexual feelings.

These three patterns of communication – the double-bind, the 'me first' and the un-hearing – are common patterns in families experiencing some distress. It is important to note some characteristic features of these patterns. The first is that the communication follows some rule or set of rules.

These rules relate both to the nature of the communication – to the *pattern* – and to who is affected by the operation of the rule. In our double-bind example, the process rule is that two conflicting messages are delivered to the eldest son: the 'victim' rule is that the son always loses when double-binds are in play. In the 'me first' example, Sheelagh's process rule is always to communicate her own importance and her 'victim' rule is that her sister should lose; however, since her sister is also playing this particular game, both lose. In the un-hearing example, the process rule is that whenever a particular subject (homosexuality) is raised it is deemed not to have been raised and John is the losing victim. These rules are not accidental; they are deliberate actions of family members. Though deliberate, they are not explicit rules. They have to be discerned from careful observation of family interaction patterns and by a study of the implicit feature of family communication.

The fact that the rules are implicit rather than explicit implies a further feature of these communication patterns – a feature of particular importance to those seeking to help a family member or a family experiencing distress. It concerns what happens if the rule is confronted. Families using the kind of patterns we describe here frequently deny that such rules exist; indeed, in many cases (see Hayley, 1959) even the 'victim' of the rule seeks to deny its existence. Such is the collectivity of families. Yet this denial of the existence of rules is itself a family rule.

This last observation leads to an interesting proposition, namely that a person within a family who feels that a rule exists and always operates against his or her own interest also feels that there is no way in which he or she can identify the rule to others without reinforcing his or her own position within a family as 'victim'. As Pelazzoli *et al.* (1978) observe, such a person recognizes at one and the same time that a complex game is being played within the family: the first rule is that there are no rules; the second rule is that he or she loses, and the third rule is that he or she cannot stop the game being played. Indeed, authors such as Laing, Bateson and Pelazzoli suggest that, in the light of such a game-plan, it is not surprising that some family members in the families most proficient at this game become schizophrenic.

To illustrate this complex idea, consider the situation of Mr and Mrs Hobbstone. Mr Hobbstone is convinced that his wife will always suspect him of resentment towards her since he thinks that she is unable to cope with even slight criticism – she seems to believe that her husband's criticism is a first sign that their marriage is not working. If he talks with her about his feelings, she will take this as implying criticism of her, and thus create resentment between him and her. So he keeps quiet, becoming more and more resentful that he is unable to share a feeling that he has about his wife and their relationship. Mr Hobbstone is a good example of a person who, feeling that something is not right in his relationship, also feels unable to confront the issue honestly, since it is his wife's refusal to accept honest comment that is the cause of his initial feeling. Mr Hobbstone chooses not to act on his feeling since he feels that the emotional costs of talking about it are greater than the costs of not talking about it at all.

What has been said so far is not all that surprising. It is that communication in families takes place in particular patterns according to rules. Who sets the rules and who therefore decides who is to be the 'victim' of such a rule will vary from family to family. What is interesting to ask is why such rules exist in the first place. There are essentially two reasons. The first concerns the extent to which the rules seek to reveal to family members and others how cohesive and adaptable the family is. The second concerns roles within the family.

Cohesion

In looking at a family's communication pattern it is possible to discern how 'connected' individuals within that family are. Put another way, communication patterns are indicative of the types of relationship that exist within a family; such relationships reveal the extent of cohesion within a family. Understanding cohesion within a family is important for those seeking to help families in distress for two reasons. First, it reveals the extent to which the family as a whole versus some subgroup within the family is distressed. Second, it suggests to the helper the extent to which he or she will need to orient his or her work towards the family as a whole, one of its subgroups or an individual within the family in order to alleviate or modify the distressing experiences. (More will be said about subgroupings within families below.)

Minuchin *et al.* (1978) suggest that there are four levels of cohesiveness within a family. At one extreme, a family can be said to be *enmeshed*. This term is meant to imply that the family is tightly interlocking – all actions and communications by one family member are met by actions and responses from another. Whenever something happens which is stressful to one member, the stress is experienced by others within the family acting in sympathy with that person. Whilst individuals within the family may, from time to time, feel like freeing themselves from the 'burdens' of other family members, they are incapable of doing so, since the nature of the family is like a spider's web that holds them in connection to others also in the web. At the other extreme of cohesiveness is the family best described as *detached*. In this type of family there are few communication connections between family members. Stress felt by one member is not necessarily felt or noticed by another. The family home is more of a complex lodging place for family members. The mother, in particular, experiences this type of family as distressing – typically she feels exploited by other members of the family, feels frustrated in her own ambitions and needs and has a low image of herself and her abilities and (not surprisingly) often presents physical symptoms of this distress to the family in the form of psychosomatic disorders. Minuchin and others suggest that these two types of family are more likely to experience distress than other types of family, since their internal structure leads to distress.

Murgatroyd and Apter (1984) document a detached family in action, and we present their case study here as an illustration of how distress can be generated within a family of this type:

1 Jake (aged 12) presents a problem: he expresses fears about school and develops a variety of physical symptoms which make his attendance at school impractical.
2 Mother moves to protect Jake against criticism from the rest of the family, especially Father, who openly threatens him with no more spending money unless he sorts himself out and gets back to school.
3 Mother is laughed at by both Sue (daughter) and Father. Father laughs openly at Mother for treating Jake like a baby and says that she is helping him avoid school by encouraging him to remain ill.
4 Mother reacts to these taunts physically and she becomes depressed – she is hospitalized for the physical illness.
5 Father runs the family home and runs it with more fun and 'verve' than Mother. Jake is well within 24 hours and returns to school and stays there without illness for the two weeks Mother is in hospital; Father, Jake and Sue do things together (e.g. shopping, watching TV, going to the park) in ways which are not done when Mother is at home.
6 Mother recovers, returns home and takes over the management of the household.
7 Father withdraws; he becomes bored and restless and depressed;

he smokes and drinks more than usual and becomes argumentative with other family members, especially with Sue about her dress, Jake about school and Mother about everything.
8   Jake shows signs of physical illness and seeks to find excuses for not going to school.
9   Mother moves in to protect Jake.
10 The family goes back to stage 2 above – the cycle recommences.

Though under certain circumstances (e.g. between stages 3 and 6 inclusive) the structure of this family changes, when complete the family is detached and each individual seeks to use some strategy (illness, argument, depression) to maintain his or her presence within the family. While this is a complex case, it is indicative of the kinds of distressful communication patterns that emerge in such families.

In addition to these two extreme types of family – enmeshed and detached – Minuchin identifies two other types of family cohesion systems. The first of these types is *connected* – here family members feel that they are in tune with each other, but not governed by the feelings and actions of others. Though involved with each other, they are not dependent upon each other for their emotional life. They are connected rather than enmeshed; concerned for rather than dependent upon other members of the family; and anxious to ensure the well-being of other members without becoming so involved that they are taken over by the feelings and thoughts of others.

The final type identified is referred to as *separated*. In this type, family members have some limited involvement with others, but essentially feel and act as individuals within the family rather than as a collective. They are separated rather than detached – implying some better connection between them than is the case with the detached family.

In thinking about these four types – enmeshed, connected, separated and detached – it is useful to consider them as a dimension. At one pole there is enmeshment, representing a very high level of cohesion, whilst at the opposing pole is disengagement. Healthy family functioning is most often associated with the two middle positions – connected and separated – and distress with the extremes. That this is so is confirmed by some research evidence (Sprenkle and Olson, 1978; Russell, 1979).

Apart from our illustration of the detached family, the ideas presented so far in this section have been very theoretical. To give these ideas more practical value we offer two descriptions of families which have presented themselves to us as helpers during the last two years. In doing so we seek to highlight the value of our interpretation of their cohesiveness for the practice of helping.

The Williams family Mr and Mrs Williams are extremely wealthy (he is known to be a multimillionaire). They live in luxurious surroundings and have several cars, a swimming pool, a private teacher for their daughter 'so that she won't have to mix with the riff-raff down the road' and several house-helpers (servants). Their daughter (Sharon) is 17 years old. On her 17th birthday her father gives her £2000 and tells her that the days of free hand-outs are over – she will have to manage her own life from now on. The mother knew nothing of the father's intention until she read in a local newspaper that her husband had published a legal announcement disclaiming any liability for the debts of his daughter. The first the daughter knew of her father's decision about her future was when she arrived home after a weekend with friends to find all her clothes packed ready for her and a car loaded with her other possessions.

Through the course of a discussion with a helper which was initiated by the daughter's attempted suicide and the mother's depression, it emerged that the three of them had not spent more than 20 minutes solely in each others' company for three years. The mother claimed she did not understand her daughter; the father claimed he did not understand either his daughter or his wife; and the daughter claimed that she did not understand her parents or her own feelings and that she felt alone. Further exploration revealed that the description 'being alone' was suited to each member of the family. It also revealed that there were only two points at which some kind of family engagement could be detected. The first concerned animals – all members of the family had a passion for animals (especially horses) and could enjoy conversations and shared experiences which revolved around animals; the other was a fear that friendships were not genuine – people befriended them because of their wealth.

The detachment within this family was almost total and was symbolized by the public disengagement of father and daughter (via the press announcement). The helper explained that what had happened was that Sharon had been chosen to symbolize the disengagement of the family as a whole. Sharon was not being asked to 'go and make it on her own as her father had done' simply because this is what the daughters of millionaires do, but because this was an inevitable consequence of the family's pattern of contact. The father had helped to bring the family together, albeit in a distressing way, by his actions; for the first time in a good many years mother, father and daughter were talking to each other in an honest and emotional way. The helper asked if they wished to continue to be detached or to help each other become more connected. The fears of each member of the family about becoming 'more connected' were explored and the family is still together at this time.

The Haydn family Jack and June Haydn are successful business people with a moderate income. They have two sons – Paul (aged five) and Arnold (23 months). Paul has developed a severe stammer and has nose-bleeds occasionally. Whenever Paul has nose-bleeds, Arnold develops cholic and Jack has migraines. In describing her elder son's difficulties and the related family illnesses, June has started to speak so fast that she stumbles over words and confuses names and illnesses – much to the amusement of family friends. They seek psychological help with Paul's stammering and the helper asks to see the family as a whole.

The family had not seen the various illnesses and symptoms as being connected in any way. When it is suggested to them that the symptoms they each develop are essentially symbolic of the way in which the family shows support and connectedness for a family member who is experiencing some distress (Paul), then they begin to see other forms of simultaneous connections which emerge from time to time in the family.

Further exploration reveals that Paul's nose-bleeds occur whenever June and Jack are arguing (usually about some trivial matter). The helper compliments Paul on using the nose-bleeds as a way of drawing the attention of the family to the danger of becoming disconnected through argument. The family begin to work on the idea that the nose-bleeds are a product of their interaction, not of any medical abnormality. They accept that the nose-bleeds are a way of a child saying that he wants the family to stay connected and that the related symptoms of others are also reinforcing this message.

(It should be noted here that the psychologist was involved following a detailed medical examination of Paul which showed that his nose-bleeds were not due to some medical problem.)

These two case illustrations (presented very briefly here) show the difference between the detached and enmeshed ends of the dimension of cohesiveness with which we are here concerned. They also show the use of a particular helping technique, that of *positive connotation*. In each of these two illustrations, the helper seeks to change the understanding of the distress the family is experiencing by providing a positive way of thinking about the function of that distress. Nose-bleeds are not 'a problem', but a symbol of the family's connectedness; the father's public disengagement from his daughter is a device for bringing the family together. This technique is derived from the work of Mara Pelazzoli and her co-workers (Pelazzoli *et al.*, 1978) and depends for its success on the helper having (a) an understanding of the structure of the family in terms of cohesion and (b) an insight into the positive role that some seemingly negative event has in relation to this structure. What is interesting about this procedure is that it depends crucially upon the helper's accurate understanding of the cohesiveness of the family – it requires the helper to have some hypothesis about the nature of the family's communication pattern before it can be used effectively.

To illustrate the value of positive connotation, consider the case described by Murgatroyd *et al.* (1985) of the 18 year old young man who has a stammer and is in the sales force of a large company. The family seeks help to 'cure' the incurable stammer since they feel it will impair their son's promotion prospects within the company. Instead of seeking to modify the speech behaviour of this young man, the helper offers the family a positive connotation: the stammer is actually an advantage to the salesman. First, it defies the image of the 'slick' and 'sharp' salesman; second, it provides a strong compelling reason for those he is trying to sell to to listen carefully to this person who has a mild and not uninteresting disability. In this situation a change in the young man's speech disability is not seen to be possible and yet a change occurs: a disability is reframed, regarded in a positive light and becomes an advantage. For this positive reframing to occur, the helper needs some insight into the motives of the family in seeking help (to show support and connectedness for a family member) and a hypothesis about how an apparent negative feature is in some way positive. We shall return to further examples of positive connotation and reframing later in this chapter.

Adaptability

Cohesiveness is one feature of the family which the helper needs to attend to when trying to understand the communication system adopted (implicitly) by a family. Another such feature is *adaptability*, also identified by Minuchin (1974). Adaptability in this context means the ability of the family to respond to a challenge or change. The challenges and changes referred to in this context can come from external sources (e.g. unemployment, changes in social structure, some external event such as illness) or from internal sources (e.g. normal development, self-development and the personal impact of some educational activity). What the helper needs to look at is the characteristic family pattern of coping with changes.

In looking at this feature of the family two general points need to be borne in mind. First, the way in which families cope with certain events (e.g. bereavement) is in part determined by social convention (see Murgatroyd and Woolfe, 1982). In the case of bereavement, for example, social conventions in England and Wales suggest that mourning is appropriate (rather than relief), sadness should be experienced (rather than joy) and black should be worn (rather than any other colour). In contrast, the social conventions of parts of rural Ireland suggest that, in bereavement, sadness should be followed by some rejoicing at the release of the soul of the dead person, that laughter at past memory is as appropriate as sadness over the recent death, and so on. In one country the wake is a (declining) convention whilst in another the black–sad mourning is a convention. The helper therefore needs to be aware of the extent to which a family's responses are culturally appropriate. (This last point is especially important for those working with families in a multicultural community.) The second point is that the helper working in a family focused way needs to examine the family model of adaptability, not simply the collection of individual coping strategies adopted by the individuals within the family. The question the helper needs to ask is: what does the family *as a family* do when faced with challenge or change? The role of each individual is important in answering this question, but the question requires the helper to look above and beyond the actions of individuals within the family.

Minuchin again offers four descriptions of forms of adaptability that can be used to form an adaptability dimension. At one extreme he identifies the *chaotic* family who, when faced with some change, all respond in different and contradictory ways. For example, a family faced with a severe financial problem which responds in this way may have an elder daughter who resolves some of her own feelings by spending money, a mother who refuses to spend money on essentials, a father who abandons any attempt to solve the problem and a son who steals money in order to help the family. The actions of any one member exacerbate the problem faced by the family as a whole whilst at the same time having contradictory effects. Indeed, the behaviour of this family in the face of serious financial difficulty can be characterized as being both disorganized and fruitless: whatever the mother saves is squandered by the daughter and whenever the father tries to avoid the issue his son, the behaviour of his wife and the actions of his daughter confront him with the problem.

At the other extreme of this dimension of adaptability is the *rigid* response. No matter what the difficulty is that the family experiences its members always respond in the same way. For example, one rigid response is that the family is unaffected by the event that challenges it. In their work on the impact of unemployment upon the family (reported in Murgatroyd and Woolfe, 1982), Murgatroyd and Shooter describe the case of a family whose members behave as if the loss of work by the father (the sole wage earner in the family) has no impact upon them. They continue to drive a car, to entertain friends, to take Continental holidays; indeed, so complete is this rigid 'maintenance of sameness' that the father still leaves the house and returns as if he was keeping normal working hours – in fact he spends his time in libraries, cafes and a working man's club.

Between the two extremes of chaotic and rigid responses to change, two other responses to challenge used by families are documented by Minuchin. The first of these is *flexible* – the family *as a family* reviews the situation, examines options and tries out a strategy; if this fails the family then reviews the situation again, explores alternatives and embarks upon a different strategy. This process continues until the difficulty is resolved: the members of the family review and adapt according to circumstances but do so collectively. The second of these 'middle-ground' responses is referred to as *standard*. In this model, the family has a restricted repertoire of responses to change or challenge which its members use in sequence until they feel comfortable with the outcome. The number of strategies in the family repertoire is likely to be restricted and the important feature of this problem is that the same sequence of responses tends to be used, whatever the situation. The family, because it knows the sequence of strategies to be tried, acts on an implicit basis – very little is made explicit and the family does not act as collectively as in the flexible response pattern just described.

We have provided brief illustrations of the extremes of this dimension – the cases of family finance and of unemployment. To make clear the middle positions on this dimension we now provide two case illustrations of the flexible and standard responses. In doing so we again seek to highlight the role of the helper.

The Jackson family   Sonya (aged 34) and Mike (aged 29) have two children, Jake (10 years) and Tracy (six years). Sonya wants to work and Mike already has a job. The questions the family members faced, and did not at first agree on, were twofold: (a) Would the child care arrangements that they would have to make affect the family in any way? (b) If they felt that the child care they opted for would affect the children, what were the implications of this realization for Sonya and Mike?

The problem was first tackled by Sonya and Mike: they talked to friends who had faced this problem and collected information about the local services they could use; they drew up a list of options that they faced and costed and looked at each of them. They then talked to their children about what Sonya was thinking of doing and Tracy seemed most unhappy. Sonya went to visit a local support group for women returning to work with Tracy and Tracy met some of the other children involved in their scheme for afterschool child care. Tracy did not like the arrangements and instead preferred being looked after by a specific aunty, to whom she was very close. Mike and Sonya approached the aunty and she agreed (in exchange for payment) to look after the two children during the school term between the end of school and the time Sonya returned from work. Tracy agreed to go to the support group centre during the school holidays.

In looking at these arrangements Mike felt that he wanted to explore the likely impact on their marriage of Sonya working. A helper at the support group came to visit the family and spent two hours exploring the feelings of all of them (Tracy and Jake included) about Sonya returning to work. Later the helper spent two hours with Sonya and Mike alone exploring each others' feelings about the change in the pattern of their domestic life and relationship that might result from the decision Sonya was now making.

After three months, Sonya and Mike asked to see the helper again to resolve some anxiety both had about the impact of Sonya and Mike's work pattern on the family.

In this illustration, Sonya and Mike, with their children, explore flexibly the options which face them and seek help to resolve uncertainty (their help-seeking behaviour here is a further sign of their flexibility). They revise their plans in the light of reactions and are not afraid to seek further help once they have implemented some change strategy. A rigid response from Mike would prevent Sonya working, whilst a chaotic response from both Sonya and Mike might soon lead to all family members being distressed.

The Gurman family   Mike and Mary Gurman are both 43 and have three children: Sally is 15, Mike is 16 and Bert is 11. Recently they have had to face up to two separate problems. The first concerns Sally – she has started to have intercourse with boys of her own age and has 'shocked' her parents by her sexual behaviour. The second problem is that Mike (the father) has taken a job which will involve him being away from home for three months of each year, leaving the family in the care of Mary. Both of these are regarded as significant problems by Mike and Mary.

The first response to both problems is to seek information about the resources in the community that can help – family planning clinic, health centre, doctor in the case of Sally; relatives and friends in the case of Mary's need for support during Mike's absence. Having collected information on these points, Mike and Mary discuss them, with Mary making most of the decisions. They then talk to all the children together and subsequently to each child separately, telling them of the decision they have made. They then stick to their decisions.

The difference between this 'standard' family and a 'rigid' family is that there are a variety of features to their strategy: it is a sequence of events, each of which is different in character, rather than a rigid response. In contrast, a flexible family would be willing to revise decisions in the light of experience, adjust positions, involve others more directly in the taking of decisions, and so on.

To make the links between these two dimensions of cohesion and adaptability clear we offer Table 2 as a summary of the key points made in this and

Table 2 The communication and response origins of distress and relative well-being in families (after Olson et al., 1979)

Nature of family interaction	→	Problem-solving and coping	→	Personal or emotional consequences
Enmeshed		Chaotic		Distress
Enmeshed		Rigid		Distress
Separated		Flexible		Well-being
Separated		Standard		Well-being
Connected		Flexible		Well-being
Connected		Standard		Well-being
Detached		Chaotic		Distress
Detached		Rigid		Distress

the previous section. The table suggests that certain styles of family interaction (cohesion), when associated with certain forms of problem-solving and coping behaviour (adaptability), have emotional and personal consequences. Some of the positions in which a family can find itself (e.g. enmeshed/rigid or detached/chaotic) are more likely to lead to distress than others (i.e. connected/flexible). Although it is a bald statement of some complex ideas, Table 2 may be useful for the helper to keep in his or her mind's eye when working in a family focused way.

The point to notice about the two dimensions of adaptability and cohesion introduced by Minuchin and refined by others is that they both concern the implicit features of communication within a family. In order for the family system to operate effectively within the terms of one of the categories, family members have to understand the implicit rules of communication within that family. For example, a family behaving in a rigid way when faced with some change will be unwelcoming of a family member's attempts to encourage flexibility; a family which is enmeshed will not readily agree to the desire of one member to become less connected and more disengaged. These 'frames' (used here as in picture frames) within which the family works are made up of communications (verbal and nonverbal) as described earlier in this chapter. Family members caught in one frame and who desire to be in another will experience some distress; families in one frame (e.g. rigid or chaotic) and who desire to be in another but lack the wherewithal to move will also experience distress. The distress will be more acute if the frame the family is experiencing is at the extremes of the cohesion or adaptability dimensions described here.

From the helper's viewpoint, these two dimensions − adaptability and cohesion − provide a broad framework for understanding the communications within the family. The kinds of questions that helpers might ask in the light of these descriptions are: What do the patterns of interaction that are described or observed tell the helper about the adaptability or cohesiveness of the family? What information does the helper need in order to formulate a hypothesis about the framework of the family's communication pattern? What insights and hypotheses about distress can be derived from an understanding of the position of the family on the two dimensions described here? What does thinking about family communications in terms of these two dimensions lead to in terms of helping strategies? This last question will be returned to later in this chapter. The point to note here is simply that communications within families need to be examined in terms of some simple framework if the helper is not to be 'lost' in the pattern of possible interpretations. The two dimensions described here are valuable in analysing the positions of families.

Roles and Subgroups

The previous two sections described in detail the two features of family communications – cohesion and adaptability – which a number of workers (especially Minuchin) regard as valuable for the helper's understanding of family communication. Also introduced in the penultimate section were the ideas of positive connotation and reframing, these being specific devices which helpers can use for their interventions in families. In this section we introduce two more features of family communication – the ideas of roles and of subgroupings – so as to further refine the ideas we have developed here. The theme is still communication in families, but we are especially concerned here with the concept of roles and rituals.

If it is possible to discern the pattern of cohesion in a family – as it is in the case illustrations of the Williams and Haydn families – then it is possible for the helper to ask what part each family member plays in perpetuating the communication pattern of the family. For example, in the Williams family, is the mother always responsive to initiatives taken by the father – does she ever initiate any action without the father's foreknowledge? In the Haydn family, when did the mother initiate any family activity which did not involve either family consent or her husband's foreknowledge? What would happen in the Williams family if Sharon (their daughter) did exactly what her father had asked and left home to 'fend for herself' and was pleased to do so? Did Sharon's father act in the way he did in the full and certain knowledge that Sharon and her mother would react in the way that they did?

The study of family communications reveals very clearly that family members enact roles in a systematic way as a feature of their daily life. A role is defined here as a ritual patterning of relationships within a family, such that the way person A always behaves towards person B in the family is, to some extent, predictable. (This definition does not suggest that all aspects of the relationship between A and B are predictable but rather that many such features are.)

What does this mean in terms of understanding family behaviour? First of all it means that a family's interactions (especially when dealing with a problem over which the family feels strongly) are likely to indicate role assumptions. In the case of the Jacksons, documented earlier, both parents act collectively – the role description that could be provided for their behaviour is one of mutuality; in the Williams family the father initiates and mother and daughter respond. In fact, exploring the nature of the relationships between Mr and Mrs Williams and Mr and Mrs Jackson reveals this to be a general description of their roles in the family's communication system. Other roles commonly observed by helpers include the following: (a) the eldest teenage daughter taking over and challenging the mother's position in the family as carer, such that the mother feels a need to restore her position (conflict) or to accept defeat (resignation); (b) the eldest son challenging the position of the father in the home as leader of the family 'group', such that the father feels a need to challenge the son (fight) or resigns his position (resignation) – a situation increasingly seen in those families where the father is no longer a wage earner but the eldest son is; (c) an older son or daughter seeks to exert authority over a younger son or daughter, resulting in some rivalry or conflict between them; (d) the father being nurturing towards other members of the family whilst the mother is confronting of others or (more commonly) the mother being nurturing towards other members of the family whilst the father is more confronting; (e) the eldest son and the mother sharing a common view in opposition to the view of the eldest daughter and the father; (f) the eldest son or eldest daughter challenging the family's implicit assumptions about dress, etiquette, manners, roles and duties to the extent of being isolated within the family.

These examples are illustrations of how, in specific cases, families behave through roles. But what are the functions of the roles which family members adopt? Essentially, according to several writers (Minuchin, 1974; Liebman *et al.*, 1974), the roles adopted by family members are the means by which they are able to mark out boundaries either between themselves and others or between their group within the family and other groups. Healthy family functioning requires individual space to be recognized along with certain collective obligations; it also requires that the work of subgroups (e.g. eldest daughter and mother; eldest son and father; the children; parents) be accepted and recognized and clearly marked out. This is necessary if the implicit tension between individual autonomy and family interdependence is to be productive rather than a further source of distress. It is for this kind of reason that roles and communication rules are implicitly adopted.

The adoption of roles and rules in families is an implicit rather than an explicit feature of family life: a point given considerable emphasis in the pioneering work of Paul Watzlawick and his co-workers (Watzlawick *et al.*,

1967, 1974). For example, in enmeshed families, typical communication rules are as follows: (a) one family member speaks for all family members; (b) there is no need for all family members to speak to each other, since one or two adequately reflect the views of all; (c) any family member may answer a question addressed to another family member; (d) other family members are usually talked about when they are not present (see Jones, 1980, especially at p. 73). Also in such families, the father or the mother is empowered to speak for their children – the role of children is to follow the family 'line'. These rules and roles are not formally adopted at some annual general meeting of the family: rather, they arise out of the patterns of family interaction which each family member permits of others. By seeking to understand these roles and rules, helpers can intervene in families by firmly marking out boundaries. In the enmeshed family described here, they can insist that, during their contact time: (a) no one family member has the right to speak for all other family members, an individual is able to speak only for him- or herself; (b) each family member is entitled and encouraged to speak to each other family member, there are no limits to the possible combinations of conversation partners within the family; (c) questions or requests for information can only be responded to by those to whom the request or question is directed; and (d) family members will not be talked about unless they are present. This form of helping – confronting the implicit rules and roles – seeks to change the basis of the family's communication system such that family members are enabled to adopt new roles and rules more suited to their needs. Such an intervention is only possible following a careful scrutiny of the family in terms of the models outlined here and the helper having some clear hypothesis about the nature of the rules and roles adopted within the family.

The task of seeking to change rules by which a particular family appears to operate when the helper only has access to one family member is exceptionally difficult. Normally, the helper would seek to affect that person's understanding of the family's rules and encourage them to develop ways of subverting or changing the rules so that the rules are changed by his or her action. But this is a risky strategy, and can put tremendous strain on this one person – unduly increasing his or her distress. An alternative is for the helper to invite other family members to participate in the helping process for a specific time and a specific purpose and to use this time to work at the communication system of the family. If these additional family members do not attend, this provides the helper with some confirmation or further insight as to the nature of the family's rule system and boundaries. If they do attend, the helper has a clear opportunity to attempt to affect the communication rules of more than one family member.

Often, families are unaware that they are using implicit rules and roles when interacting with each other. If the helper develops a facility for observing these rules and roles, then he or she can often reduce distress by helping to make explicit these roles and rules. For example, the helper can ask the family to re-enact some dialogue which is indicative of their distress. Alternatively, the helper can arrange the family physically in a way which expresses the roles and rules of the family. If the father is dominant, he is asked to sit on a larger chair in the middle of the family group; if the children are generally 'left out' of family communication, they are asked to sit well away from their parents. These symbolic representations of family rules – used extensively in family sculpting and drama therapy (Duhl et al., 1973; Papp et al., 1973) – can be powerful ways of drawing the attention of all family members present to the roles and rules they have come to take for granted and which may, in themselves, be a source of distress.

The Role of Coalitions in the Family System

To this point in this chapter we have described family communication in terms of the transactions which take place between parents, between parents and their children and amongst the children within a family. But others are involved in the family – most notably, the grandparents of the children and aunts and uncles. In some distressed families the roles taken by these others is critical in shaping the family's communication system. In this section this issue is explored.

One source of distress for a family occurs when a coalition is formed between one or more members of the family and a relative of a different generation. Such coalitions, which are usually covert and denied, can occur between one parent and his or her own parents, between one child and one parent, or between the children of the family and a grandparent. For example, one parent continually joins with the children to oppose the discipline behaviour of the other parent. In this example a coalition is formed across a generational boundary so as to inhibit the actions of a particular parent. A second example of a cross-generational coalition occurs when a grandparent becomes over-involved with the children and in so doing undermines the position of the parents. In this last example, the children pose a problem for the parents in that they have to choose between two different ways of behaving – that suggested by the parents and that suggested by the grandparent.

A final illustration concerns the invitation to one child to take on a parent-like role in the family in a kind of 'marriage' with one parent which makes the other parent feel incompetent or unwanted. The common characteristic of these examples is that some alliance or coalition is formed across generational boundaries in such a way as to create the potential for distress.

Another way of thinking about this form of coalition, which we stress is usually covert and denied, is to think in terms of boundaries. The boundaries within a family are structured by generation from youngest to oldest – children, parents, aunts and uncles, grandparents and great-grandparents. In families which are not distressed the boundaries between these different levels of generations are clearly marked and understood. Children are clear as to the status and role of grandparents versus parents; parents are clear about their roles in respect of the children and are able to differentiate their roles from those of their own parents. In distressed families it is often the case that some feature of the generational boundaries is obscured or confused and that roles are not clearly marked out.

To make this point clear, here is a case illustration from our recent experience which documents a particular form of such coalitions.

The Jermin family The Jermin family consists of Mike (35), Mary (37), June (16) and Tony (12). It is a very close family. Each weekday one of the grandparents (Mike's mother), who lives close by, visits the family as the children arrive home from school. She has done this since June was eight. Since both parents work, the grandmother was seen to be providing a valuable function for the family.

Recently, June has been the source of a great deal of conflict in the home. She has dressed in a manner unacceptable to her parents; has used language they find offensive; has been seen partly clothed with a boy in the park – all behaviour which Mike and Mary find unacceptable. Most recently she has been involved in glue-sniffing.

In the course of the second session with a helper it became clear that a major influence on June's life was her grandmother. Her grandmother had encouraged her to experiment with life. Whenever she tried something – sex, dressing up, glue, – her grandmother would explain that she had the right to experiment with her life, but that she ought to think carefully about the consequences of what she was doing. Grandmother made clear her disapproval of the things she actually experimented with (especially the glue-sniffing), but continued to encourage her to experiment with herself – to find out more about who she was. The parents knew nothing of this.

When the parents faced the grandmother with the suggestion that she had encouraged the daughter to behave in this way she denied it, saying that what she meant was quite different from what the girl was now suggesting. By 'experiment' she meant that she should not make hasty decisions about her future (men, jobs, education) but instead should experiment with these features more than her parents had done. The girl denied that grandmother had talked in this way.

This situation, unusual though some features of it may seem, is symbolic of the kinds of implicit coalitions that emerge when generational boundaries are crossed. The consequences here are serious for the family. In exploring them it soon became clear that the grandmother felt strongly that her daughter-in-law should not be working and should be looking after her children *as she had had to do when she was a mother*. The helper's intervention highlighted this conflict of values and encouraged its resolution in a way that was acceptable to the family, after some emotional outpourings of feeling.

The case illustration of the Jermin family is used here as an example of the consequences of an illicit coalition within a family. Other examples could have been given which have a less dramatic outcome. The point for the helper to note here is that they need to examine the way in which others are involved in the family and the perceptions which family members have of this involvement.

The Symptom Carrier

A specific role within a family's communication system is taken by the person displaying most distress. Rarely do families present themselves to helpers as a unit. It is normally some individual within the family who is displaying more distress than others which gives rise to the family making contact or being referred to a helper. The person displaying the 'symptom' (we use this word for convenience here and do not imply by its use any medical assumption about the nature of distress) is referred to as the symptom carrier or (more commonly in family therapy) the identified person or client or patient. In this brief section we wish to explain the role of the symptom carrier in the family and the importance of this person for the helper.

The symptom carrier's major role in the family is to highlight the distress the family as a whole is experiencing. Seeing the bedwetting child or the glue-sniffer as an individual with a personal problem is one option the helper has; another is to recognize the importance of that person to the family and to see his or her behaviour as both personally distressing and a powerful symbol of the family's distress. To make such an interpretation work the helper needs to have an understanding (or hypothesis) about the nature of the family (in terms of cohesion and adaptability, the respective roles of family members and the roles, if any, of outsiders) and needs to be able to think about the positive way in which the behaviour of the identified person can be interpreted by the family (what we have called positive connotation).

The suggestion that the helper needs to find a way of offering a positive interpretation of the behaviour of the symptom carrier is not always easy to follow. Families resist the idea that what they have hitherto found distressing or disturbing is suddenly of value. Yet this resistance has to be confronted by a helper who seeks to convince them that the symptom carrier has provided a valuable service to the family in, for example, highlighting unresolved issues; bringing the family together; opening out discussion of matters to other members of the family. If the helper is seeking to affect significantly the communication patterns of the family, such a positive connotation is a necessary step.

One practice that often helps in understanding the role of the identified person in the family is for this person to be seen alone by the helper. This is then followed by a session in which other family members are seen by the helper and then a further session in which all family members are seen together. Such a practice is commonplace in the work of educational psychologists. The purpose of this procedure is to establish the different frameworks within which different family members view the actions of the identified person. This enables the helper to consider the different viewpoints of all concerned and to formulate some way of highlighting the positive feature of the behaviour of the person who is the focus of the family's attention.

Whether this procedure or some other method is used by the helper to gain time to understand the positive feature of the distress behaviour, it is important that the helper does not passively accept the definition of the distress of the symptom carrier offered by the family. For, as a moment's thought will confirm, the family's definition of its 'problem' begins from the family members' own assumptions about the kind of family they comprise; if the helper accepts that the behaviour of the identified person arises in part out of the kind of family it is, then it follows that he or she should be cautious in accepting the definitions of the situation offered by the family.

The Role of the Helper

Throughout this chapter several comments have been made about the role of the helper. It has been suggested that: (a) the helper needs to be a critical observer of the family's communication and interaction patterns so that he or she can make some judgements about the family he or she is dealing with; (b) the helper might need to confront the implicit rules of family communication or the roles taken by specific family members; (c) the helper might need to offer a positive connotation or a reframing of the distress shown by the identified person (symptom carrier) in order that some development might take place; and (d) the helper will need to attend to the role played in family life by those in the family hierarchy who do not live in the family household (e.g. aunts, uncles and grandparents). In this penultimate section of this chapter we explore in some detail the role which helpers might play in reducing the distress experienced by a family.

Before beginning this task it is worth noting that a number of the interventions suggested to this point make assumptions about how many family members the helper has access to. If communication patterns are to be changed through the role of the helper, then it is most desirable that as many members of the family as possible are involved in the process of helping. In part this is because the helper is thus enabled to observe more directly the communication patterns of family members. In part it is because the rules of family communication are best confronted when those most associated with the rules are engaged in the confrontation process. But the involvement of the whole family in the helping process is not always possible or practical. The helper needs, therefore, to interpret the suggestions made in this and earlier sections in the light of his or her own helping relationships with a particular family.

A related point is important here too. The ideas developed in this section, like those presented earlier, depend for their success on the helper feeling confident in their use. We are not offering in this text prescriptions for helping or statements about what ought to happen. Rather, our aim is to provide some ideas and frameworks against which helpers can consider their own practices. Equally important to this section of the chapter is the need to recognize that the skills and processes associated with the phasing of helping we now describe depend upon the helper effectively communicating the core conditions of empathy, warmth and genuineness (see the Preface at page xi and Chapter 7 at pages 139–40. In pursuing these features of the helping process the helper will be sensitive to the minute by minute needs of those with whom he or she is working and will adjust, modify or abandon the 'helping phase' which he or she is then engaged in so as to attend to other needs which arise. Thus in outlining helping phases here we do not imply a series of mechanical, preprogrammed steps, but rather a framework for the helper to use when engaging in the task of family focused work.

What follows is a description of a number of phases of helping activity. These phases vary in length and form from family to family and from helper to helper. They are offered here merely as a way of structuring the ideas for helping which result from an understanding of rules, roles and hierarchies within families.

The first and most critical feature of a helping approach aimed at changing or significantly affecting family communications and roles requires the helper to observe those members of the family who are involved in the helping process engaged in the act of communicating. Often this takes place when the family members are describing to the helper why it is they are seeking help. Sometimes helpers (especially social workers, educational psychologists, education welfare officers, health visitors, doctors and probation service workers) are able to build up a picture of family communication as a result of continued involvement with a particular family over time. In other cases it may be necessary to set the family some task – e.g. documenting the events of the last few months which have given rise to some distress in the family – so that the process of communication can be observed directly. A great many of the practical suggestions which follow require the helper to show confidence in his or her developing judgement about the styles of interaction, cohesion and adaptability of the family whilst at the same time being willing to revise his or her judgement in the light of evidence and testimony. In a sense, the helper's strategy depends upon having a hypothesis about the kind of family being worked with. This hypothesis does not need to be very sophisticated – we are not suggesting that the observation phase of helping needs to last several weeks – but it is important that the helper establishes the starting point for his or her understanding of the nature of family communications in the terms outlined in this chapter as quickly as possible. It is equally important that the helper revisits this starting point and revises the working assumptions in the light of change, development, new insight or evidence concerning the veracity of earlier views. Helping is a dynamic rather than dogmatic process.

The next phase of helping involves the helper in drawing the attention of family members to the implicit communication rules within the family and to the roles played by specific family members. Three particular helping actions are used in a variety of forms of helping. These are as follows: (a) blocking normal patterns of communication within the family and suggesting alternatives; (b) emphasizing differences between family members in terms of both what they say and how they say it; and (c) making explicit any implicit conflicts between family members. Let us examine each of these activities in a little more detail.

Blocking normal transaction patterns is a standard helping procedure. For example, in several families we have seen, questions addressed to children are answered for them by their parents. Blocking this transaction requires the helper to insist that a question addressed to a particular person is answered by that person. Another example is when an unfinished statement is offered by a family member (e.g. the person does not seem able to end his or her statement) and another family member offers an interpretation to the helper of the form 'What X really meant to say was . . .'. By insisting that each person can speak for him- or herself, the helper blocks a transaction aimed at reinterpreting the view held by one member in the terms offered by another.

Emphasizing differences involves the helper in drawing the attention of the family members present to the (sometimes subtle) differences of meaning and interpretation of some event or problem by different family members. For example, in the Weston family the son (Brian, aged 12) plays truant from school and has been caught stealing from his mother's purse. Brian says he does this because he is bored; his father says Brian does this because his mother doesn't provide enough for Brian to do and she doesn't give him the encouragement he needs over his school work; his mother says that Brian picks up these bad habits from the gang he associates with at school. The mother and father in this case agree that Brian is 'a problem'; Brian says his parents are a problem because they are not interested in him. In talking about these different views, it soon becomes clear that the same words (especially 'bored', 'support', 'stimulation', 'interest') are being used in different ways by each of these three people. The educational psychologist involved in this family worked for a little while at identifying the different ways in which these words were being used by family members and highlighted the essential conflicts between them as a result.

To make explicit the conflicts in the family the helper needs first to be trusted as a helper by the family and second to be sure that the conflicts which he or she is highlighting actually do exist in the family: the minute the family loses confidence in the helper who is using this strategy, the strategy will fail. At several points in this chapter it has been suggested that conflicts within families are often implicit rather than explicit. In the case of the Jermin family (see page 54), for example, the conflict between the values of the grandmother and those of the parents was implicit in the situation rather than explicit. They only became explicit when June's behaviour led the family to examine critically the reason for June's behaviour. The role of the helper in this case was to highlight the conflict of values and its consequences for the family. Other ways of performing this task involve the helper taking sides with one group against another within the family or the helper establishing a rule that highlights the conflict(s) within the family (e.g. one group shall always disagree with the views of another group within the family, whatever these views are).

These particular helping practices have two consequences. The first is that they substantially increase the distress the family experiences, though usually only for a short time. Whilst many helpers would resist these processes for precisely this reason, others (see Minuchin and Fishman, 1981, in particular) argue that increasing the distress a family experiences by confronting their implicit communication patterns and roles and making them explicit is essential if the helper is seeking to affect these patterns and roles. Much depends upon the kinds of difficulty the family is experiencing – the helper needs to decide upon the appropriateness of these practices to the needs which he or she has identified in the family. But this is where the second consequence of these practices arises. It is that the helper puts him- or herself 'on the line' when engaging in them. By this we mean that a helper who uses one or other of these techniques is doing two things: (a) making explicit his or her assumptions about the family's communication patterns and roles; (b) putting his or her credibility as a helper at stake. The first of these points highlights the value of the observation phase and the second reminds us that a great deal of helper activity involves the helper in making a judgement and then living with the consequences of that judgement in terms of the work with the family.

A related feature of the helping process aimed at changing the communications, interactions or boundaries of a family in distress can take a variety of forms. We document two here. Both concern the way in which the helper seeks to use the symptoms of distress in order to highlight the nature of the family's implicit rules, roles or hierarchies. The first is positive connotation, which has been mentioned at several points in this chapter. Briefly, positive connotation involves the helper in reinterpreting the distress of the symptom carrier in positive terms (see pages 43 and 44 for further details). The purpose of this is to offer the family an alternative way of conceptualizing its current experience. As an alternative, many helpers make use of what is known as *paradoxical intention* or paradox for short. The basic idea of paradox is to exaggerate some feature of the family so as to confront the family with this feature in a way which requires them to change. Three examples will make the point more clearly.

Example 1 A young boy (aged nine) is brought to the health centre by both parents because he gets angry when he doesn't get what he wants – the parents think this might be a sign of some psychological disturbance. The psychologist suggests to the child that there are more situations in his life that he can show anger over and suggests in the strongest possible terms that, rather than showing less anger, the child ought to show more and lists some 30 situations (e.g. when his breakfast is not ready when he wants it, when his father has not left his pocket money out for him, when the television programme he would like to see is not being shown) in which the child should (according to the psychologist) show anger. The result is that the child now rarely behaves in an angry way. There are just too many situations defined as appropriate by the psychologist for the child to react to – he would be angry at all times if he followed the directives offered by the psychologist. (This work was undertaken with the collusion of the parents.)

Example 2 John (33) has a severe stutter and his wife Anne (27) is concerned that their young child, Mike (seven months), will learn to stutter from his father. They seek help to 'cure' John's stuttering. Rather than seeking to train John to speak without stuttering the doctor asked John to stutter all the time, not just some of the time, and to exaggerate his stutter as much as he could. When faced with this instruction John soon (within six days) found himself stuttering only rarely. The instruction to stutter more made John stutter less.

Example 3 A couple were experiencing sexual problems which were having an effect on the rest of their family life – both were irritable and agitated and frequently rowed and argued. The children felt that they were being victimized within the family for a reason they knew nothing about. The problem was the husband's premature ejaculation. The marriage guidance counsellor the couple went to see asked John how much time was involved between the erection occurring and ejaculation taking place; John and his wife estimated that it was about three minutes. The counsellor suggested that John aimed to get this time down to less than a minute and gave him a stopwatch to time himself accurately. It was explained to John that this task would demonstrate clearly whether the problem was something John could control or whether the problem might need some medical investigation. John tried to do as the helper requested and found that the time between erection and ejaculation actually increased to over seven minutes and that on subsequent occasions the time increased rather than decreased. In this case a command to reduce an activity increased the activity.

The common feature of these examples of the helper's use of paradoxical intention is that the person in distress is asked to continue that distress in a more exaggerated form in which the problem is made the solution; the very fact that this instruction is issued makes it difficult for the individual to continue to perform this task. Full descriptions of this process can be found in, for example, Watzlawick et al. (1967, 1974), Frankl (1963), Barker (1980) and in many standard texts on family work (e.g. Jones, 1980).

Many helpers will be rightly cautious about using paradoxical intention in their work. It requires the helper to take a considerable risk in terms of the relationship he or she has built with those he or she is helping, though the risk is reduced by careful observation and assessment. It also puts the helper in a position of having to manipulate those he or she is helping, which some will find unacceptable. None the less, paradoxical intention is a specific form of using the 'symptoms' of distress displayed by the identified person.

All of these processes, to be successful, require the helper to have built trust and acceptance into the relationship with those he or she is helping. As Hayley (1976) observes, successful helping along the lines outlined here requires the following: (a) the existence of a trusting, sensitive and communicative helping relationship – an imperative to the success of all family focused work; (b) a clearly defined problem where the definition of the problem is based on observation; (c) the existence of clear goals in the mind of the helper; (d) a statement to the family about the reasons for the helper's actions – especially important in the case of paradoxical intention; (e) a clear statement to the family members of the work, idea or task they are being asked to perform; (f) careful monitoring and understanding of the responses of the family and their use by the helper as a basis for revising his or her view of the family; finally, (g) attribution of credit for change or improvement not to the helper but, instead, to the family. In thinking about the phases and processes outlined here, helpers would do well to bear in mind Hayley's comments (Hayley, 1976).

One final point here: families experiencing distress are skilled at incorporating helpers into their system of communication. Helpers need to be mindful of this fact and need to take care that their involvement in the family is planned and subject to their own self-critical scrutiny: becoming absorbed into the family's communication system can mean that the helper becomes a part of the family's problem rather than a part of the solution to their problem.

Conclusion

This has been a long and extensive chapter which has sought to examine the ways in which the communication system of a family and the roles adopted by family members can be seen as sources of distress. In addition, we have outlined some helping roles which are appropriate if the helper is seeking to affect in some substantial way the communication or role system operating within a family. The ideas here are complicated and involved, though we have tried throughout to illuminate them with practical examples and case illustrations. This chapter forms an important background to other sections of this book, since some of the ideas introduced are highly relevant to the material appearing under other chapter headings. If readers are searching for a summarizing phrase for the ideas of this chapter, we offer this: a family showing signs of distress is a family with a distressing pattern of interaction; to reduce the distress the helper needs to affect the patterns of interaction, and this is no easy task. Subsequent chapters present alternative ways of considering the task of the helper.

4

TRANSFERENCE, PROJECTION AND INSIGHT – FEATURES OF THE PSYCHOANALYTIC TRADITION

Introduction

Perhaps more than any other school of helping, the psychoanalytical tradition has been associated with an individualized approach to persons in need, though, as we shall suggest, there is no necessary reason why this should be the case. Indeed, in many ways the psychodynamic method used in this tradition is well suited to family focused work and has consistently been employed as such. Its relevance is well expressed by Pincus and Dare (1978) who refer to 'the unconscious network of feelings, attitudes, wishes, beliefs, longings, fears and expectations, that link family members to each other and to their past lives and past families'. The way in which psychoanalytical therapists incorporate the family into their work is also articulated by one of the tradition's major exponents, Winnicott, who describes the balance of the individual's inner life and the family environment in the following way: 'each individual child by healthy emotional growth and by the development of his or her personality in a satisfactory way, promotes the family and the family atmosphere. The parents, in their efforts to build a family, benefit from the sum of the integrative tendencies of the individual children' (Winnicott, 1956, p. 47). In this same work, Winnicott describes (p. 48) how, in assessing a child's suitability for psychotherapy, attention is paid to the family's willingness and capacity to 'tolerate' and to 'hold' the child during the period of therapy. Certainly according to its own practitioners, psychodynamic methodology is consistent with and well suited to an approach which concentrates on families rather than individuals. We have no reason to argue with this assessment.

In this chapter we examine some of the basic ideas of psychoanalysis as used in family focused work. In particular, the concepts of repression, transference, projection and insight are used within some broad principles to highlight the nature of the helping process. Illustrative material from our own case work and that of others is used to illuminate the value of the ideas explored for the helper. Throughout, the concern is to share and make relevant some ideas about the origins of distress and the process of helping. The work associated with this chapter is influenced strongly by the writings of Pincus and Dare (1978), Framo (1972, 1976) and Winnicott (1956). At this point a case study might usefully illustrate some of these ideas. Consider the case of the Williams family.

The Williams family The Williams family consists of father Jack, mother Jill and children Paul, aged 12, and Susan, aged 10. The presenting problem is that Paul is displaying symptoms of maladjustment at home and at school. At home he has been disruptive and staying out late. He has been truant from school and, when there, has been abusive to teachers. Susan is a quiet girl regarded as a bit 'introverted' at school. The parents lead a calm and ordered life. Mr Williams works as a clerk, while his wife is a shop assistant. In his leisure time he does a lot of gardening while she goes out to the Women's Institute once a week. Beneath the family calm, however, there is a lot of anger. Both Jack and Jill come from families in which there was a great deal of overt conflict. Jack's parents separated when he was five and his mother married again to a man whom he never liked. Jack's reaction was to keep a low profile and stay out of sight. Similarly, in response to violence between her father and mother Jill went to a lot of after-school clubs plus the Girl Guides and generally kept away from home as much as possible. In both cases, the reaction to violence was to retreat from it. This pattern is reflected in their own marriage. Underlying conflicts about sex (Jack's desire is much stronger than Jill's) and about money (Jill thinks Jack is wasteful) are suppressed and never discussed. The anger in this relationship is repressed but finds expression in their son Paul, who becomes a scapegoat for the family's angry feelings. His 'maladjusted' behaviour only makes sense when seen in this context. As Mr and Mrs Williams are helped to see how their own angry feelings have been repressed, their relationship improves, Susan becomes more outgoing and Paul's angry behaviour recedes. What has happened in this family over the years is that feelings and unresolved conflicts have been expressed and projected in such a way that the whole family is affected, even though the presenting symptom is seen as residing in just one family member.

Origins of the Psychoanalytical Approach

The previous chapter documented the ideas that inform the schools of family focused work based around systems and communication ideas. Some of the ideas documented there are also relevant here. However, the major driving force behind the psychoanalytical tradition was Sigmund Freud and his ideas have been given impetus in family focused work by James Framo (1972, 1976). The work of Freud and of those who have contributed to the psychoanalytical literature since Freud is complex and extensive. It is not possible in the space available here to offer a detailed description of all features of psychoanalytical theory and the psychodynamic helping process or to outline the origins of the various ideas and procedures. Readers interested in the history of these ideas or in fuller descriptions and in contemporary applications will find materials by Framo (1965, 1976) and Boszormenyi-Nagy and Framo (1965) helpful. Generalized introductions are provided by Jones (1980) and by Barker (1980).

The Principles of the Psychodynamic Approach

In their study of marriage, Pincus and Dare (1978) suggest that there are four general principles, which they say represent ways of looking at relationships. These principles are as follows:

(a) *People's motives for getting married are largely unconscious* By this they mean that the conscious or articulated motive represents only a part of each individual and that behind the conscious choice lies a complex web of needs, desires and fantasies. Helping couples, therefore, involves looking at the whole person, including helping them to get in touch with that part of themselves which is not allowed to surface to consciousness as well as that which does.

(b) *In marital relationships 'there is usually a mutuality and complimentarity in the needs, longings and fears that operate in the partnership'* (Pincus and Dare, 1978, p. 37)   It follows, therefore, that the notion of blame is alien to the helping process and that if a relationship is unsatisfactory or distressing the contribution of both marriage partners has to be examined. What one can say is that there is usually a collusion as to the unconscious elements of the relationship. Projection is an important concept here. By this idea we mean that what is found to be too painful to accept in ourselves is projected outwards on to some other person. A useful exercise aimed at understanding projection is to focus upon a person or persons with whom one does not get on well and to ask how far this is because that person displays some quality which is present in the subject himself or herself but is too painful to allow to surface into the conscious mind. As a result it is projected outwards on to some other person. Much marital conflict can be explained in these terms. For example, David is frightened to display aggression and subconsciously chooses an aggressive partner to carry that aggression for him. He then discovers that he doesn't like Joan because she is aggressive. Reciprocally, Alice, a dominant woman, has selected a quiet mate, Peter, who can carry those more reflective qualities she would like but is unable to locate in herself. She then comes to a helper complaining about what she sees as Peter's lack of aggression or over-passive qualities. In this way, we can say that the two people collude in their projections, a collusion which takes place not at a conscious but at an unconscious level. We shall say more about projection later in this chapter.

(c) *Many of the patterns of unconscious fears and conflicts that are present in the marital relationship are derived from earlier childhood relationships*   For example, Arthur, who comes from a strict moral background in which his father was an invalid and his mother had to work hard to make ends meet, marries Margaret, whom he perceives as sexually attractive, but who in practice turns out to be rather frigid and to be ambitious and dominating. Arthur then finds himself doing the domestic chores while Margaret goes away on business. He feels inadequate in relation to her and sorry for himself just as he felt sorry for his inadequate father. What has happened is that his parents' relationship has been almost, one could say, compulsively re-enacted, with himself cast in the role of victim.

(d) *The most powerful formative period for each individual is that known as the Oedipal phase* This is the time when 'the little child can realize something of the intensity of his own longings towards his parents whilst at the same time recognizing that the parents are themselves a couple with a particular and potentially intense relationship with each other from which the child is excluded' (Pincus and Dare, 1978, p. 39). It is at this period that the developing child most intensely experiences the relationship between two adults, which, therefore, strongly influences his or her own adult relationships.

The past is important in the psychoanalytic approach in that past experiences are seen as having a strong influence upon present relationships. In a review of family therapy practices, Speed (1984) describes this as 'an object relations approach, where the relationships learned in interaction in childhood are seen to be internalized and carried forward into later relationships'. In this way we can say that past experiences shape present behaviour. Note that we deliberately use the term 'shape' rather than 'determine'. Speed suggests that practitioners trained in the psychoanalytic approach have generated 'a view of the family as an interacting whole . . . with . . . emphasis on the therapist's understanding of family members' inner experiences and feelings, fantasies and projections and how these interrelate in the family matrix'. The idea of wholeness is vividly illustrated in the title of Skynner's book *One Flesh: Separate Persons* (Skynner, 1976). Speed suggests that these practitioners in family therapy (whose training often involves psychoanalysis) have maintained first 'an awareness of the individual within the interactional whole' and secondly 'an historical developmental perspective' which takes account of the individual emotional histories of all family members. She compares this approach with that of practitioners lacking in psychoanalytic training who 'tend to have been more dismissive of the significance of the individual and the individual's relationship to the whole; have concentrated more exclusively on the here-and-now of the family and its problems' and minimize the importance of earlier learning as a precursor to present distress. Speed's own view is that 'the connections between the individual's inner world, individual behaviour, interaction and system, i.e. interlocking patterns at all levels, are crucial'. Readers will recognize the congruence with our own position: that the social structure, the social world which individuals inhabit, has to be considered in any attempt to understand the roles and relationships people play and the emotional repertoires which accompany these roles and relationships.

Speed's position is similar to that taken by Framo (1972), Walrond-Skinner (1976) and Eaton et al. (1976). Their view is that mental events (such as the feeling of being distressed) do not occur at random but have their origins in the history and experience of the individual. Put succinctly, the past is always a part of the present. Most critical events that shape the emotional life of a person have some root in childhood experience.

Simon Simon, aged 16, was referred by his school to the clinical psychologist. He was regarded as a bright boy with an excellent opportunity of getting to university. His school career had been marked by hard work and solid achievement. He was popular with his peers and with teachers. Yet suddenly he became sullen and withdrawn, stopped doing homework and announced his intention of leaving school and finding a job. There was no apparent reason for his change in attitude and behaviour. As the helper worked with Simon it became apparent that he had undergone considerable pain at the death of this father three years ago and that his feeling of loss had not been fully expressed. Simon had been expected to be strong and as the eldest child to give emotional support to his mother and younger brother. It transpired that, about six months ago, the parent of one of Simon's friends had also died and this event and his friend's reaction to it had re-activated or triggered these same repressed feelings in Simon. Because they were too painful for him to allow them to surface completely to consciousness, they had become manifested in the form of depression. With the helper's aid, Simon was able to share his feelings of sadness and anger and loss with his mother and younger brother and was soon adopting a more purposive attitude towards his life. His relationships with his mother and brother also improved.

The Freudian Model

To understand these ideas more fully it is necessary to have some elementary understanding of Freud's model of the personality. Freud distinguished three territories of the mind: the id, the ego and the superego.

The 'id' is comprised of those mental processes associated with 'drives' or motives. Amongst many motives individuals have for their activity, the psychoanalytic tradition gives emphasis to sexual drives (libidinal drives) and aggressive drives. The id has two psychological functions. The first is to satisfy the person's sexual and aggressive drives. The second is to maintain equilibrium in the person so that tension can be minimized or reduced. From this point of view, distress occurs *either* when some needs are not being satisfied *or* when the id is failing in its attempts to reduce the psychological tension a person experiences. In a family, there are many features which are tension producing and anxiety provoking – if the individual is unable to regulate this tension then distress will be experienced.

The 'ego' serves a different psychological function from the 'id'. The ego seeks to organize memories and thoughts into some pattern which appears logical to the person. In organizing these patterns the ego seeks to find some compromise between what the id desires (e.g the fantasies and phantasies which result from the various drives which the person has) and what is realistically attainable in a given situation. In pursuing this task of modifying the desires of the id in the light of the relationships and environment in which the person finds themselves, the ego works at both a conscious and unconscious level. It is through the ego that the person views the world, perceives his or her relationships with others, makes judgements and offers explanations for his or her behaviour. It is through the ego that we view both ourselves and others. In the context of family life, the ego modifies any sexual desires a father may have for a daughter or the mother has for a son and converts such desires into terms of endearment acceptable to other family members. Another example of the functioning of the ego concerns the way in which parents discipline disobedient children: in some cases the 'id' may seek to be very aggressive with such a child, but the ego normally manages to modify this aggression such that the punishment administered by the parent is deemed to be appropriate to the level of disobedience of the child. In exercising this function, the ego makes considerable use of both the conscious and unconscious memory of the person. In the example given, the ego calls upon those moments in the person's life when his or her parents showed some sexual or aggressive interest in that person as a child and this memory informs their action. When the ego fails to operate in this way incest or child abuse may be seen to occur – the ego performs a basic self-regulatory function in the person's own life and in his or her interaction with other family members.

The 'superego' is more generally referred to as 'conscience'. Its role in the individual's psychological life is to provide the individual with a sense of moral value and, in so doing, ensure that the individual experiences guilt whenever he or she transgresses his or her own values. Put another way, the superego is that part of our psychological being which provides us with the standards by which we conduct our lives; when we break these standards it is the superego which encourages feelings of guilt. The superego is in part a function of child and adolescent development. Prior to the development of a superego the child feels very little guilt – though he or she may 'behave themselves', it is more normally for fear of punishment by parents than because he or she refrains from some act because he or she disapproves of it. Also important in the development of the superego are the social and moral values of parents and the community in which they live. In the context of family focused helping this description of the superego makes clear why it is important for the helper to try to connect current distress to both present experiences and past events. For distress arising from a dominant superego the source will normally have its roots in the past. It should be emphasized here that the superego is essentially unconscious – it only becomes conscious when we feel ourselves to be transgressing some ideal standard we have of ourselves.

This brief description of Freud's basic model of the personality indicates how anxiety (which is what generates a desire for change) can occur. Anxiety occurs because of a conflict between the instinctual desire of the id and the practical and moral positions taken by the ego and the superego. Two examples will illustrate this. The first is of Albert, a father in a family of four who continually has a desire for extramarital sexual relationships: although he does not actively pursue this desire, he always feels that one day he might. His wife Helen is aware of the tension that this gives rise to, most especially when they are in the company of a large number of people. Their 'solution' to this problem is to minimize the number of occasions when they go out together – this they see as a device to minimize temptation. Since both are gregarious and fun-seeking this decision (never openly decided but which has operated for a considerable time) actually leads to both of them being frustrated and irritable; this in turn increases the strength of Albert's desire. Here the desire (id) is cautioned by the superego and the ego produces a practical solution, but in so doing increases the tension and anxiety felt by both partners and this threatens their marital relationship.

A second example concerns the desire of a young mother, Eve, to have more children, even though she is aware that the family does not have the financial resources to support any additions and that her husband Eric finds children very difficult to live with – at the moment they have only one child.

The result of this is that Eve seeks out sexual activity with Eric but is continually anxious about the prospect of pregnancy, despite the fact that her husband always uses a sheath. As a result of this anxiety, Eric complains about Eve's sexual performance and is himself becoming anxious about their sexual activity, though for different reasons. In this complex situation the ids and egos of this couple are interacting in different ways to produce marital tension which is focused around sexuality (for the husband) and a desire for children (for the wife).

People who experience anxiety often do so at an unconscious level; it is not always clear to them what the anxiety relates to or how this anxiety comes about. Conflicts between id-wishes and ego or superego demands are often complex. One way a person handles such conflicts is known in the psychoanalytic tradition as *repression* – the person excludes from their conscious mind any knowledge related to this conflict which they find difficult to deal with. Repression is difficult because the id continues to try to have its wishes satisfied. To maintain repression and keep difficult inner conflict in the unconscious, the person makes considerable use of *defence mechanisms*.

The purpose of defence mechanisms is threefold. First, a defence mechanism is used to minimize anxiety. By placing into the unconscious a previously conscious and disturbing idea, memory or desire the person seeks to reduce feelings of conflict and anxiety. Second, a defence mechanism is used to protect the ego. Placing into the unconscious some feature that has been disturbing the person restores his or her ability to function through the ego in the real world. A failure to protect the ego's functioning could make it more difficult for the person to behave in an acceptable way in the family. The final function of a defence mechanism is to maintain repression. If repression is not maintained then the person will experience greater anxiety and distress since the conflict between id-wishes and ego or superego demands will have been revived. Some of the defence mechanisms typically used to reduce anxiety and distress are denial and displacement. Through denial the person is able to reframe his or her experience in a way that excludes him or her from having a part in creating that experience. Through displacement the person is able to relocate the experience in another setting – anxiety which arises at work and which he or she does not feel able to affect is displaced on to the family, where the person feels more able to control the situation. All defence mechanisms are unconscious devices that ward off distress and anxiety. They are valuable ways of reducing distress when they work well. When they do not work well they create their own distress over and above that engendered by the original id–ego or id–superego conflict.

These comments on the basic structure of the personality seek to introduce some key elements of Freudian psychoanalytical theory. Later sections in this chapter will introduce other related concepts – especially projection, transference and counter-transference. But now we need to examine the implications of these ideas for the practice of helping.

The Role of the Helper

We have entitled this section 'the role of the helper' but readers will be aware that psychoanalytic theory would employ the concept 'therapist' and the person being helped would be referred to as the 'patient'. This is more than just an academic niggle. The term 'therapist' derives from the European psychoanalytic school and implies a relationship between helper and 'patient' (the person in need) containing a strong element of authority such as is symbolized in the parent–child relationship. In contrast the term 'client' derives from a less crisis-centred, more developmental orientation. American in origin, it emphasizes working with people in a client-centred fashion. It places more emphasis on the 'here and now' (immediacy) of the relationship between helper and client. Our own preference is for the term 'helper' (see Murgatroyd and Woolfe, 1982), which moves us away from the idea of a professional doing something to a client and incorporates a wide range of approaches to helping people. However, we do accept and acknowledge that many readers would be happier with a more specific term implying a range of professional skills, such as 'counsellor', although, as we have pointed out, the psychoanalytical tradition would refer to the 'therapist'. In this context it is interesting that the Marriage Guidance Council, working empirically within a mixed psychodynamic and humanistic framework, prefers to refer to its helpers as 'counsellors'. The point of this discussion is to indicate how concepts are not merely the nuts and bolts of methodology, but contain within them the ideological structure which underlies helping practice. Pursuing this line of approach further, readers may well feel that the term 'client' should also be questioned as implying dependence and replaced perhaps by the idea of 'consumer' (using a service) or even 'punter' (taking a chance). These suggestions are not totally light-hearted; however, we do not wish to pursue them in this text.

Transference

The aim of the helper is to help the person in need to gain an insight into him- or herself and his or her relationships. The quality of the relationship between the person in need and the helper is a crucial component in this task. This raises a series of questions about what helpers do, how the work proceeds and what position is taken in relation to the person in need. The psychoanalytic tradition stresses the importance of such questions to such an extent that some of its central concepts, particularly 'transference' and 'counter-transference' are concerned precisely with this area of activity. When people come for help the 'symptoms' presented to the helper may be sexual, or they may be problems over money or time or intergenerational conflict, or they may take the form of a more diffuse form of quarelling. But whatever the 'symptom', the role of the helper is to look for the 'fit' between members of the family and to look at the relationship of the family as a whole in terms of the family as a system. To do this the helper must first perceive of him- or herself as a crucial element in the equation. It is often said that helping others begins with the self of the helper and it can be argued that, whatever the school of counselling or therapy, the most critical factor in producing a successful outcome to the process is the nature of the helper–client relationship. Nowhere is this more crucial than in the psychoanalytic tradition. This relationship does not take place as if on a clean slate but is influenced by our past interactions. In the words of Storr (1979, p. 69), 'we do not approach new people as if they were blank sheets, but "transfer" what we have already experienced from the past into the present'.

Storr believes that this process is particularly important in helping for two reasons: the first is the 'maintenance by the therapist of comparative anonymity' and neutrality; the second is that 'since the patient is asking for help, he is, automatically and inescapably, in the position of regarding the therapist as an authority' (Storr, 1979, pp. 69–70). Storr adds that in his view

> 'transference, (and I am now using the term in its widest sense, that is, as comprising the whole gamut of the changing relationship between the patient and the therapist) is the most important single factor in therapy. For what the therapist tries to do is to understand and interpret the patient's attitude to him, and by this means to help the patient understand his difficulties in relationships with others' (Storr, 1979, p. 71).

Without too much doubt, change is unlikely to take place in the client unless positive transference exists between client and helper. The concept of transference refers to the extent to which images of past relationships are generated by a relationship in the 'here and now' (present); that is to say there is a transfer of feelings from one relationship to another. So if, for example, a client perceives images of a loved parent in his or her helper, those images may be transferred to the helper and thus the person is more likely to work successfully with that helper than if they had perceived images of a hated parent and the transference had been negative. Reciprocally, the helper who sees in a client echoes of another person about whom negative images exist may transfer these images to the client and this may be inimical to developing a positive helping relationship. The term 'countertransference' is often used to describe the helper's perception of or response to the client, but is sometimes employed specifically to refer to a neurotic (anxious) response. For example, a helper who is aware of some unease in his or her dealings with gay (homosexual) clients may have reason to ask if there is some area of his or her own sexuality that has been blocked off from awareness. So far as the implications for helping are concerned, the main need is for the helper to be aware of the existence of negative transference. If this exists, then it is important for it to be brought to the surface and to be discussed between the helper and the client. This not only helps the relationship to continue, but more purposefully may be a useful focus around which the client can examine areas of conflict or 'stuck' feelings which are causing distress. Negative transference is not a disaster for the helping relationship and can indeed offer a potential basis from which the helping process can advance.

Recently recruited helpers sometimes make the mistake of shying from negative feelings either because they themselves are frightened of such feelings in themselves (like anger, frustration or dislike) or because they sense that the expression of such feelings would be inimical to the helping process. Clients often come for help precisely because they are unable to express negative feelings and for the helper to be able to express his or her own feelings (negative or positive) is itself an important component of helping. It indicates to the client that expression of feeling is possible without destroying a relationship or losing self-esteem. The more the helper is able to express negative feelings the more the client is helped to unravel areas of feeling which have become blocked. One of us, for example, recently worked with a client, Richard, whose reaction to the slightest stress was to retreat. The helper pointed out to him that if he did this to some very mild questions it was hardly surprising that he had found his wife Denise's sexual advances threatening. The helper also pointed out that he felt snubbed and ignored by the client's constant withdrawal. The expression of these angry feelings in a considered way was actually appreciated by the client, who began for the first time to see how his withdrawal was affecting other people, especially his wife. The careful expression of anger was, therefore, a therapeutic tool of some value, which helped to unblock the client's 'stuck' feelings and made him more aware of his own contribution to his sexual and relationship problems. Paradoxically the more the helper is able to express negative feelings, the more prized clients may feel. They begin to feel that if their helper values them enough to reveal feelings which are clearly honest and profound and difficult to express rather than glib and superficial, the helper's feelings towards them must be generally positive. The helper cares for them enough to be honest and genuine with them. Helpers should of course be sensitive to the difference between 'reaction' and 'response'. The latter is instinctive and spontaneous and is sometimes helpful, but the helper has to be aware of what the client can take and in what form. Often the expression of negative feelings like anger is best expressed in a more deliberate way (responding rather than reacting). Banging one's fist on the table is not the only way of expressing anger.

The Helper as Parent and Adult

Another useful way in which to perceive the client–helper relationship is in terms of a process involving child, parent and adult relationships. The ideas of parent, child and adult states, derived from transactional analysis (itself derived from the psychoanalytic tradition), offer us a conceptual framework within which to examine this process. Helpers often find that clients, both as individuals and as families, come for help with unreal expectations. For example, they believe that the helper will offer them a fairly direct form of help, guidance, instruction and advice. In doing so they see themselves as equivalent to a deficient child in need of knowledge which the helper as a parental figure possesses. In crisis work, particularly where there are likely to be few meetings between helper and client, this is precisely what may characterize the relationship – it is a fairly direct relationship in which advice is given and received (see Chapter 6). In a longer-term helping relationship, it may be necessary for the helper to encourage the client to see that what he or she can offer is not advice but an ability to help the client to explore the areas of pain and conflict, so that he or she is better able to make decisions for him- or herself – a more non-directive, facilitative approach. In this situation, the relationship is less that of parent–child than of one adult talking to and working with another adult. While this mode is dominant within the humanistic model of helping, it would be perceived within the psychodynamic tradition less as a working model than as a desired end product. In this perception, the process of helping may indeed involve taking the person or persons being helped through childhood conflicts in such a potentially pain-filled way that the favoured relationship (perhaps the only way in which the client will feel safe enough to expose himself or herself) is that in which the therapist is seen as a nurturing parental figure and the client's childlike regression is not just accepted but regarded as an integral aspect of the therapy. As the therapy proceeds, the relationship moves into a more adult–adult form of transaction.

This discussion of the process of helping within the psychoanalytical tradition is very much in terms of an ideal type and in reality helpers will be aware that the process of helping is a much more heterogeneous one. For example, some clients have never experienced fully adult relationships with another person and for the helper to maintain such people in their childlike state simply perpetuates old and established patterns. To offer the client the opportunity to form a reasonable relationship with the helper on an adult–adult basis may, by that very fact alone, be the most positive feature of the helping process. We give as an example here the case of the nervous unassertive man, Geoff, who arrives for help because his wife Brenda has left him unexpectedly. During the early phase of helping he reveals that he came from a home in which his father was an invalid, his elder brother joined a seminary, and most of his own interactions at school with adult males were with priests. It seemed hardly surprising, therefore, that his model of masculine behaviour and emotions is vague and poorly developed. Being helped by another man who was not from this background offered him the opportunity, seemingly for the first time, to see that he is capable of forming a mature relationship with another male; this relationship then offered him the opportunity for some elementary but valuable modelling of behaviour.

The Process

What this discussion tells the helper is that the first questions to ask him- or herself about the client are: What is happening in the helping relationship right now? What effect am I having on the client? How does he (she, they) perceive me? What is or are the client or clients doing to me? How am I being affected by them? If a helping relationship seems to be proceeding well and progress is being made, such questions tend to be left implicit and there is no pressing need to raise them with the client, but if the relationship is blocked, they must be explored in a conscious and adult fashion. Now this is often quite difficult. For instance, one of us was recently presented with a female client, Norma, whom he found very sexually attractive. At first he found it difficult to see beyond the outward appearance into the rather sad little girl figure who lay beyond. For her part the client had a long history of emotionally 'seducing' male persons: father, lovers, helpers, so that they would take her side, collude with her, not want to lose her and, in so doing, ensure that she could avoid having to be confronted with any need to accept responsibility for her own feelings. In this case the fact that the helper was able to talk about his sexual attraction facilitated insight into her seduction 'game' and was a key factor in helping this person to re-evaluate her attitude towards and relationships with men, which was the primary cause of her coming for help in the first place. The helper–client relationship represented an analogue of her relationships in the real world. This example, of course, illustrates not just the importance of the helper–client relationship, but also the importance of setting the client's behaviour in the present into the context of her past experiences. In this particular case the relationship between the client and her father was a crucial contributing factor to her problems in the present. So much time and energy was devoted to meeting *his* emotional needs that she had never felt like a cherished child. Indeed the only way to get his attention had been to seduce him emotionally.

Insight

Central to all psychodynamic approaches to helping is the idea of insight. Essentially this means that the method of unravelling emotional conflict and easing pain lies in a process of introspection or looking inwards. This is clearly contrastable with a behaviourist approach (explored more fully in Chapter 5) in which the emphasis is on observed and overt behaviour. While the latter offers a ready outlet for action and change in terms of developing social skills, the former is more frustrating in the sense that awareness is difficult to define other than in the most subjective manner. Moreover, it is difficult to know what to do when one has found insights. Many helpers from many backgrounds will be only too well aware of the family whose response to their help is, 'OK, we've now got some insight or awareness into what led to our present difficulties; we can see that we are too aggressive/ passive, or controlled/spontaneous, or rigid/anarchic, etc., and that it would help us if we could move to a different point on the continuum, but how do we go about it?' There is no simple answer to this question other than that awareness is itself a first step along the road to change, i.e. awareness *is* change and that awareness is more than just an intellectual event, but involves an emotional process of owning one's own feelings. So, for example, to say that one is aggressive may have little effect if that knowledge is only held consciously (in the intellect) while subconsciously there is a strong emotional resistance to accepting the fact (accepting those feelings of anger and aggression as part of oneself – owning them). While humanistic approaches would place an emphasis on getting in touch with previously disowned feelings so that they become more readily acknowledged as one's own, helpers working in the psychoanalytical tradition would be more willing, and would perhaps even regard as necessary and desirable, that family members be offered an interpretation of their feelings and thoughts. The helper is, therefore, involved in a somewhat more directive form of helping. However, within the psychodynamic tradition, interpretation also relates to the need to help the client understand what is happening in the relationship between him or her and the helper. Storr (1979, p. 73) points out that because transference projections originate in childhood they are apt to be 'unrealistic and exaggerated' and, therefore, it is important for the helper to deal gently with the client who feels that the helper is equivalent in some senses to his or her parent(s) as the only person in the world who understands them. In other words, although the helper may be elevated into a parental figure, the process of helping the client to move into a more adult–adult relationship is one that takes time and should not be completed precipitately. This point is also relevant to the question of ending counselling relationships, which we discuss fully in the final chapter. In terms of family focused helping, while the helper working within the psychoanalytic tradition may work with the person identified by the family as in need of help, this would be perceived, as we have pointed out in both Chapter 1 and Chapter 3, as the basis of an attempt to create an experience in which the family's defences and transference processes are exposed. In other words, while the work may concentrate on one person the family itself is perceived as the focus of the problem.

Projection

In the helping process the concept of projection is of particular relevance and value to the helper. The term refers to one of the classical defence mechanisms identified by Freud. By the use of projection it is asserted that aspects of ourselves which we find too painful to acknowledge are disowned and projected on to other people. For example, the person who is threatened or frightened by his or her own angry feelings will observe these in others but not in him- or herself. A useful exercise is to ask yourself to list the people with whom you do not get on well at work (or in your social life). Now against each name, list the emotional qualities which these people possess which you do not like. Now do a third and much harder task, which is to ask yourself how far each of these qualities are ones which deep down characterize yourself. The chances are that many *will* describe you, but that because you do not like them in yourself, you have disowned them and see them only in others. This exercise is also useful in reverse. That is to say, ask yourself what qualities in yourself other people at work (or in your social life) find difficult to accept. If you reflect on this list, you may well come to the conclusion that you are threatening to or perhaps disliked by some others, precisely because you are expressing or carrying feelings for them, emotions which they find too dangerous to acknowledge consciously in themselves. This knowledge may well help you to manage such relationships in a more satisfactory fashion.

Marriage is particularly amenable to this kind of analysis. What we can say is that marriage represents a 'fit' between two people, a system in which each partner carries some of the other's emotional luggage. As an example, consider the instance of the dominant woman Diana and the weak man Charles. Charles comes to the helper complaining of Diana's unwillingness to let him go out with his friends, do his own thing, be himself. Yet he married Diana precisely because he found independence threatening. She thus carried this burden for him. He seems now to be unaware of the fact that his emotional needs now are somewhat different from what they were when he met and married her. He has forgotten what attracted him to her, if indeed he ever knew. Conversely she was attracted to Charles because he wasn't a macho or aggressive male. What she probably wasn't aware of was that he carried those qualities of passivity which she found difficult to accept in herself. Now Diana sees only the dissatisfied spouse.

The task of the helper in this situation is to help these people to recognize the unacknowledged and unconscious projections and to come to terms with these disowned parts of 'self'. The object is to help the client see that while these parts may have been consciously disowned, subconsciously they are extremely active and powerful motivating forces. The process of working towards this understanding is likely to involve clients in a reappraisal of their experiences, from childhood to their present state. What this process often reveals is a remarkable continuity of emotional and relationship patterns. Consider the case of Bob and Freda as an illustration of these points.

Bob and Freda Bob and Freda have been married for six years and they are both in their mid-thirties with no children. Bob, who comes alone to see the counsellor, announces that *he* has a problem, namely that his sexual desire is less than that of his wife. This is causing severe marital problems. The counsellor helps Bob to look at sex in the context of the whole relationship and eventually to perceive the problem as *theirs* rather than his. Eventually Freda becomes involved. She emerges as a woman who puts a lot of pressure on Bob, both sexually and in other ways. She herself was emotionally pressured in childhood when her emotional needs were subordinated to the task of meeting those of her parents. Bob is a quiet, rather passive man whose fear of failure is rooted in some rather unhappy childhood experiences in which he was expected to achieve educationally, but was denied love and affection. As both partners become aware of the sources of their present feelings (Freda of her aggression and Bob of his fear of failure) they become more aware of the effect they have on each other. Gradually the degree of emotional intimacy between them increases and, along with this, their sex life becomes more harmonious.

These comments about the helping process highlight certain features of helping which it is worthwhile to summarize here. First, helping within the psychoanalytic tradition involves the helper enabling each family member to work through those distortions (e.g. those resulting from projection, transference, and over-repression) which impair their relationships with other family members and create distress. Second, working through such distortions involves the helper in examining with the family how past experiences (especially of parents) have helped to shape current distress. Third, these helping tasks are difficult and complex and require both time and the existence of a warm, genuine and empathic relationship between the helper and his or her clients. Finally, to achieve the tasks outlined here the helper needs to be active in the helping process – helpers need to use their insights and position to expose the role of past or present and to enable the family to release themselves of the distortions which create distress. Although concerned in part with the past, the helper's task is primarily concerned with the present (Framo, 1965, especially at p. 168) – the exploration of past events and relationships is valuable only in so far as such an exploration illuminates the present.

Whose Problem is it?

A presenting problem is often a symptom of a wider set of problems – a point made poignantly in the previous chapter. The objectified result of projection is that a couple or a family often comes to define a problem as residing in one individual. For example, George arrived alone, seeking help. The problem, he explained to the helper, was that he had little sexual drive and was generally 'a lazy bugger'. If only the helper could help him to increase his energy level on all fronts, his 'problems' would disappear. Further discussion revealed that his sexual disinterest in his wife Pat was a response to her emotional aggression; one could say she was emasculating him. His general lack of energy was also a response, in part, to her incessant, restless activity, which he found difficult to match or to be comfortable with. In this particular relationship, George carried the passivity (she had projected hers on to him) whilst Pat carried the dominance and energy (he had projected his on to her). Another relevant dimension in his situation was anger and sadness, which here can be seen as opposites. Pat carried the anger (his having been projected on to her) while George carried all the sadness (hers having been projected on to him). Basically they were both lonely people. She had been badly affected by the death of a first husband and had not worked through the grief process, whilst he had been affected by an emotionally deprived upbringing. The helper helped them to see that the problem was not *his* but *theirs* and that the way to resolve their relationship conflicts was for each of them to get in touch with those parts of themselves they had systematically repressed as a result of past experiences.

This perspective is also valid in the case of children. Sometimes helpers encounter a family in which one child is said to be maladjusted: he or she will not go to school, keeps unsocial hours, has friends which are unsatisfactory, and is destructive about the house. Close examination of family patterns reveals that the family norm is for the total repression of conflict or the display of strong emotions. All these feelings have been projected on to the one child who thus carries the burden of emotional expression and expression of conflict for the whole of the family. The task of the helper, in the psychoanalytic tradition, is to help individuals see how their own needs have become repressed and projected outwards. Thus, while the problem may be manifested in one person, its source lies in a much more complex web of past and present feelings and relationships. While at any one time the helper may work with one person or with couples or with a family as a whole, the focus needs always to be upon the family as a total system.

In an article addressed specifically to marriage guidance counsellors, Ross (1979) has listed a series of projections which help in the identification of marital interaction. Readers may well find the list of value in other contexts too. She suggests that 'all marriages are an amalgam of pairs of opposites, though partners' positions on the axes may vary at different times and in different areas of the marriage'. She suggests that we can plot clients on the axes relevant to the particular marriage and she suggests the following list: strong–weak; dominant–submissive; parental–childish; independent–dependent; giving–taking; self-denying–aggressive; nagging–sulky; fight–flight. The list is not exclusive; other axes can and do exist (e.g. controlled–spontaneous). Ross also raises the possibility of shared problems existing: for example, the man and woman who both feel insecure and lacking in self-esteem and who project their insecurity outwards on to another person (e.g. one of their children) or persons (e.g. their parents) or group (e.g. their immediate community) such that what they have in common is a feeling of being victimized or persecuted by others. This list of projections is also valuable in assisting the helper to identify his or her own unconscious identification with either or both partners. For example, the helper who is nearer the thrifty rather than the spendthrift end of the continuum may find it easier to identify with a client who manifests this characteristic as opposed to the partner who does not, and thereby runs the risk of colluding with the one against the other. Such an analysis as that offered by Ross and elaborated here helps the helper to be aware of this danger.

Another difficulty in the helping process concerns the desire of family members to maintain some equilibrium in the family system – it often appears as if the family system has an ego which seeks to maintain equilibrium and reduce family tension. When one family member changes in some important way, all other family members need to change since the family equilibrium is disturbed by change. Helpers will often observe families seeking to maintain the *status quo* despite the fact of some significant change. For example, in the Brown family, the wife had transferred anger she felt towards her father on to her husband – her working assumption about him was that he was bad and needed to be shown that he was bad. She constantly punished him, was angry with him, threw things at him. Following a period of helping the wife came to realize that her anger actually ought to be directed at her (now deceased) father. In the helping process she worked through these feelings towards her father and became gentler, more accepting and supportive towards her husband. The husband, however, expressed dissatisfaction with this development and could be seen to behave in increasingly aggressive ways so as to provoke his wife's anger – he continued to seek out this behaviour from his wife even though he had complained about it for several years. When his wife did not meet these needs he behaved towards his two children in such a way as to provoke anger from them towards him, thus restoring certain family features that existed before the process of helping began. The helper's task switched from that of exposing the transference of feelings of anger from father to husband by the mother to one of exposing the husband's defence mechanism. This case illustration shows clearly that families can and do seek to maintain equilibrium in a variety of ways.

Conclusion

We have in this chapter attempted to give some kind of flavour of what is involved in helping within the psychoanalytic tradition and to indicate that much of what passes for helping within our society draws heavily upon this tradition. As a method, therefore, the psychoanalytic tradition appears to be well suited to family focused work, and to the extent that perceptions can be shared with the parties on whom fantasies are projected, it is perhaps a more powerful tool than when used in its individualistic orientation.

5

MODIFYING BEHAVIOUR AND PROMOTING 'FAMILY LIFE SKILLS'

Introduction

A primary aim of this text is to offer those involved in helping and working with families a flavour of a variety of helping practices and schools of thought so that they can consider their own practice against the ideas and suggestions presented in this book. Our belief is that, though many helpers declare a specific allegiance to some specific school of thought (e.g. psychoanalytic), a great many more see themselves as eclectic – as using the ideas and skills from a variety of sources if they appear appropriate to the task of helping a particular family facing a particular situation at a particular time. Almost certainly, one element of the eclectic approach many will adopt is behavioural.

It is our intention here to present a statement of the basic ideas of behavioural approaches to family focused work. Though many family therapists do not work within this tradition (it is interesting that a recent review of family therapy by Speed does not examine or mention the behavioural approach – see Speed, 1984), many other family focused helpers do. For example, Yule (1984) lists several features of helping work with children in which behavioural approaches are used by social workers, education welfare officers, teachers, child care workers, probation service personnel, and educational and clinical psychologists. The list provided by Yule includes the following: (a) enuresis – urine incontinence, especially bedwetting; (b) school refusal – truancy and school phobia; (c) managing pupil behaviour in the classroom; (d) training parents in child management skills, especially in the case of children with special needs (see, for example, Raymond, 1984); (e) working with children who have a mental or physical handicap; (f) working with families and children who require the help of a medical practitioner over a medical issue, especially speech difficulties, skin disorders and sexual dysfunction. This list suggests that behavioural approaches have a wide application to family life, and we explore some of these applications in this chapter.

Before beginning the work of this chapter, it may be useful to highlight the fact that behavioural approaches have been heavily criticised and opposed by certain sections of the community of helpers and others. The criticisms that are made of behaviourism are of three kinds. The first opposes behaviourism on the grounds that it is dehumanizing. For behavioural theory suggests that, though the person is clearly using internal mental processes (e.g. thoughts, motives, reflection, memory), internal mental processes cannot be reliably observed or understood and therefore need not be taken into account when seeking to modify a person's actual behaviour. This willingness to discount the mental life of the person as significant in shaping their behaviour is thought by some to be dehumanizing (e.g. Foucault, 1954). The second criticism is that, though behavioural methods claim to be based upon a scientific approach to the person, they are in fact grossly unscientific. Indeed, Patterson et al. (1977) found that the scientific status of a great deal of the work undertaken in marital therapy by behavioural workers was grossly unsatisfactory. In particular, these and other workers (Rachman and Wilson, 1980) suggest that behavioural workers need to improve (a) their methods of assessment and (b) the way in which they measure behaviour when these methods are applied to marital or family work. A more poignant scientific point concerns not whether or not it is effective (this seems to be clearly established for certain kinds of work – see Rachman and Wilson, 1980) but the need for some scientific explanation as to why the range of behavioural methods might be so effective. The final objection is a particularly technical one: it is that it is becoming increasingly difficult to separate behavioural methods from other methods, such that it is now unclear where a behavioural approach might end and another might begin.

This last point needs some reinforcement in a text aimed at encouraging a more eclectic approach to helping. Many of the differences between the 'schools' of helping which we document in this text are in fact differences of theoretical emphasis and perspective. Such differences are often much clearer to theoreticians than to those who work with individuals and groups of family members in the field. Many of those helpers who regard themselves as primarily behavioural also use ideas and processes which they see to be derived from other traditions. For example, Bulkeley and Sahami (1984) report a case of treatment for encopresis 'using behaviour modification within a framework of systems theory'. Indeed, they say that 'in forming a hypothesis about the functioning of the family system in relation to the problem, it was found useful to employ Minuchin's concept of enmeshment and eventually a plan was made to set up a behavioural programme in combination with a brief, problem-focused strategy'. Similar comments are to be found in the work of other eclectic helpers (see, for example, Murgatroyd and Apter, 1984) who work largely from other traditions, but find behavioural approaches helpful. It is in this pragmatic spirit that we offer the material in this chapter.

One other point needs to be made at the outset of this chapter. In the course of examining a variety of behavioural approaches to helping, a number of practical steps are outlined. In presenting these steps here, a logical ordering and sequencing of the work of the helper has been undertaken. But helping is rarely 'neat and tidy' in the manner that might be suggested by such a presentation (necessary for pedagogic reasons). Nor is helping as mechanical as some behavioural texts make it seem. Helpers need to be sensitive to the needs of those they seek to help; need to respond to their situations through the core conditions of empathy, warmth and genuineness (see the Preface and also Chapter 7, pages 139–40; need to remain focused upon the issues in hand; need to show flexibility in their approach to helping. This means that many of the stages we outlined in the various helping processes documented here will be sequenced differently in different cases; will run into each other or be omitted. Helpers should regard this as both inevitable and desirable – it suggests that they are seeking to fit their helping processes to the needs of those they are helping, not these people to their processes. We wish to give emphasis to this point throughout this text.

Some Comments about Behaviourism

Behavioural helping processes stem from an understanding of the behavioural tradition within psychology. This tradition sees behaviour as the product of learning. Just as a person learns to drive or swim by responding to a stimulus and being reinforced for appropriate responses, so individuals learn to respond to some stimulus within the family in a particular way and, if reinforced for doing so, will persist in that response. This pattern of learning through stimulus, response and reinforcement applies just as much to adaptive learning (e.g. effective coping strategies) as to maladaptive learning (e.g. coping which leads to distress). Thus some writers have been able to speak of people learning to be helpless (Seligman, 1975), suggesting that a response to a particular stimulus (e.g. the experience of a loss) is to show helplessness in response and, if this is sufficiently reinforced by other family members, then the person will learn that they should show helplessness whenever they are faced with a loss.

In developing these kinds of ideas, Eysenck (1976) suggests that a behavioural approach to helping sees the symptoms of those in need as the product of learned behaviour. People learn to be distressed, depressed, to play the role of 'victim', to feel caught in a Catch 22 situation. Rather than being the product of some mentalistic process (as is implied by psychoanalytic models of the origins of distress), distress results only from maladaptive learning. The task of the helper, given this assumption, is to help the person or family group to *un*learn the maladaptive learning, to learn adaptive behaviours and, by so doing, to learn not to be distressed.

Implicit in this formulation of the nature of the origins of distress is a set of assumptions about the person in need. Whether or not the helper intends it to be the case, his or her working assumption in using the behavioural approach is that those with whom he or she is working are deficient in some way (e.g. in social skills, in decision making, in problem-solving, in assertiveness, etc.) and can be helped through some training programme to learn the skills which will help them to function more effectively and experience less distress. Whilst the behavioural approaches may incorporate simple conditioning models (e.g. contingent contracting – see below), it also uses a variety of strategies to promote the learning of adaptive skills and the unlearning of maladaptive skills.

Eysenck (1976) raises a central issue for a helper seeking to work in a family focused way. It is this: to what extent are the difficulties of those with whom I am working a product simply of maladaptive learning or a product of intrapsychic forces (e.g. the interaction of the id, ego and superego) or some combination of both? Helpers need to address this question directly for themselves before beginning to use behavioural methods as a part of their helping repertoires. The uncritical use of behavioural methods – just as is the case for the uncritical use of other methods – can lead to wholly inappropriate consequences.

From the point of view of family focused helping, the subject of this book, the family provides a natural environment for the learning of behaviour. Indeed, many writers view the family as an interlocking network of behaviours, with one family member reinforcing the behaviour of another and in so doing confirming the behaviour of a third person. In essence, the family is a 'behavioural unit', in which each person has learned how to respond to every other individual who is part of that family.

The aims of helping are outlined succinctly in the following brief quotation from Jones (1980):

'. . . behaviours of each family member are stimulated by (are a response to) behaviours of each other family member. Each family member learns various ways of responding to the behaviour of each other family member. The overall goal [of helping] is to change the contingencies of reinforcement so that family members give social reinforcement for desired behaviour instead of maladaptive behaviour.'

What is interesting about the process of reinforcement – a central feature in the learning of behaviour – is that no one needs to be aware that the reinforcement is taking place. Indeed, reinforcement is often so subtle (eye glances, slight smiles, acknowledgements which are implicit rather than explicit) that many reinforcements remain unnoticed even after repeated observation of them occurring on videotape replays. The most familiar example of the reinforcement of maladaptive behaviour is the parent who shouts at his or her child for being disruptive in the home and then seeks to engage that same child in some alternative activity. Unknowingly, this parent has reinforced the child's disruptive behaviour by providing substantial attention and then participating in the design of some new activity. The result is that the child is likely to be disruptive again. He or she has learned that disruption produces two rewards: adult attention and adult involvement. This process of unintended reinforcement has been referred to as 'accidental' or 'incidental' learning (Patterson, 1975). In the context of the whole family, such behaviour is likely to be further reinforced if one parent disagrees with the other about their responses to the child – such an argument can create excitement for the child who feels that he or she is now the focus of the family's attention (Apter and Smith, 1979).

Reinforcements, in addition to sometimes being unconscious, are also sometimes mutual or contingent. Let us illustrate this point with the example of Mr and Mrs Home and their son Ben (aged four). Whenever Ben is in a particular shop he throws a temper tantrum unless he is bought sweets or an ice-cream or a comic. His temper tantrum consists of him lying on the floor, screaming and crying until he goes blue in the face. To quieten the child, Mr and Mrs Home always succumb to buying him the particular item that has sparked the particular tantrum. Clearly, the child learns that his behaviour is appropriate since it produces the good he desires. But there is a second, contingent piece of learning: the parents learn that in order to avoid a scene they have to give in to Ben's demands. Thus, here are two pieces of related (contingent) learning that mutually support what the parents feel to be a maladaptive piece of learning.

The helper, faced with the Home family and others like them, has the task of 'breaking through the cycle of mutual reinforcement' (Jones, 1980) for maladaptive behaviour and promoting new, more adaptive learning. To do so, the helper needs to give detailed attention to the nature of the learning sequence (stimulus, response and reinforcement), its contingent features and the nature of the response. This requires the exercise of considerable sensitivity and a level of objectivity which is only possible if the helping relationship is founded upon the core conditions of empathy, warmth and genuineness and is informed by a sense of trust and confidence. Behavioural workers express these last points slightly differently. For example, they might suggest that the helpers' approval (e.g. warmth and empathy) is seen by those they are helping as necessary reinforcement for the helping process to be effective.

Behavioural Techniques

The descriptions of the behavioural techniques that follow and the case illustrations that accompany them begin from the assumption that the helper will spend some considerable time engaged in what Wolpe (1973) and many others refer to as *behavioural analysis*. That is, the helper needs to develop a clear and precise picture of the sequence of events which lead to a particular behaviour being performed and the events which follow the performance of this behaviour. This requires the helper to elicit a detailed description from family members about the nature of the behaviour in which the identified person engages and which the helper regards as symbolic of the distress the family seeks to reduce. For example, one of us recently worked with the mother, father and eldest daughter (aged 11) of a family of five (the other two children were aged two years and seven months respectively and were not involved in the helping process at the request of the parents). The problem as presented was that the daughter had started to swear a lot and was now swearing so frequently that the parents felt embarrassed to take her out in case she swore. The first task was to establish what constituted swearing behaviour for these parents and how frequently this swearing behaviour occurred. The second task was to establish precisely what happened in the response–reinforcement sequence so that the helper could understand how this behaviour came to be reinforced. The mother said quickly, 'Oh, we just ignore it' and seemed to suggest that the family negatively reinforced the swearing behaviour. When asked precisely what they did when they were ignoring their daughter's behaviour it became clear that (a) the mother looked angrily at her daughter, sighed audibly and held her head in her hands, whilst (b) the father touched the mother and made an audible sound of disapproval (usually 'ahhem' or 'tut-tut'). It seemed to the helper that these specific behaviours from the parents, slight though they might seem, were enough of a positive reinforcer for the girl to continue to use swearing as a means of showing that she was able to manipulate the behaviour of her parents. Rather than ignoring the behaviour, these parents were in fact reinforcing it. This became clear through the detailed and careful way in which the helper elicited a precise analysis of all of the behaviours involved in this case.

Sometimes, some features of the behavioural analysis will be achieved by means other than interview. The parents of a disruptive child might be asked to keep a detailed record of the frequency and duration of the disruptive events in which the child engages so that graphs can be produced of the rate of disruption. These graphs are used to determine precisely how severe the behavioural problem is and as an indication of the success of the helping process, since the recording of this information will often continue throughout the period in which the family members are receiving help.

In addition to identifying the precise behaviour to be changed and the way in which that behaviour is currently reinforced within the environment of the family, behavioural assessment also seeks to aid the helper in the identification of a programme of 'treatment'. (Notice here that behavioural workers tend to use the words 'symptom' in defining the problem to be worked on, 'treatment' in describing the process of helping, 'therapist' in describing the role of the helper and 'client' in describing the person in need. The use of these words suggests a strong affinity with the medical model, a point reinforced by the comments of Eysenck (1976) and others about the status of behavioural approaches as science.) Only through the careful and very detailed scrutiny of a particular stimulus–response–reinforcement sequence can the helper begin to determine the process by which this learning chain can be broken so that distressing behaviours can be unlearned or desired behaviours which are absent can be learned.

Some of the classical behavioural techniques which the helper might choose to include in a treatment programme are: (a) systematic desensitization; (b) modelling; (c) progressive relaxation; (d) flooding; (e) assertiveness training; (f) implosive therapy; and (g) covert conditioning. Since not all of these have found a place in family focused work, only some of them will be described here. In particular, we focus here upon desensitization, modelling and assertiveness training. More details about each of the processes listed in (a)–(g) above will be found in Goldstein and Foa (1980). Recently, especially in work with couples and families, four other techniques have been developed and documented which might properly be regarded as having their roots in the practice of behaviour modification. These are (a) contingency contracting; (b) problem-solving; (c) communication skills training; and (d) cognitive behaviour therapy. Each of these techniques will also be described and illustrated briefly here. Readers should not be unduly worried by the technical-sounding terms given to these techniques – they are in fact pragmatic processes which many will identify as strategies they are already using in one form or another. Our aim here is to demystify these techniques without belittling their value.

Systematic Desensitization

John and Eileen Jones are both aged 23 and have been married for five years. In the last two years, Eileen has failed to have an orgasm and is becoming increasingly anxious about the impact this is having upon their marriage. John is also now very concerned that he is to blame for Eileen's lack of sexual satisfaction. In addition, John is becoming very frustrated at the anxiety levels experienced by his wife during sexual activity and is finding that this anxiety is now percolating into other areas of their life.

In the behavioural analysis of John and Eileen's behaviour, it became clear that Eileen's anxiety had begun by being specific to the final phases of intercourse but had now been generalized to cover all aspects of sex. Sex talk (which John liked to engage in) now produced the same anxiety as the sex act itself. Indeed, Eileen was now so afraid of not achieving orgasm that she was reluctant to engage in the sex act itself, thereby reducing even further

her chances of achieving orgasm and increasing her overall level of anxiety – a version of the Catch 22 situation (see Chapter 3, page 36).

The helper decided that there was a need to work with both John and Eileen on a programme of *systematic desensitization* – a technique developed by Wolpe (1973) and used extensively in behavioural work, especially with those experiencing difficulties in sexual behaviour. The technique has a number of steps which we summarize briefly here, showing how these steps were applied to John and Eileen's difficulty:

Step 1 Build a helping relationship and define a helping contract (see Chapter 7). Without this relationship any attempt to promote this process is likely to be time-consuming and unproductive.

Step 2 Teach the couple progressive relaxation (Hewitt, 1982) – this is a self-administered way to reduce muscle tension. It is called progressive relaxation since the couple will learn in a series of progressive steps how to relax more and more muscles in their body and how to do so under different time pressures. Indeed, it is possible to learn to relax the body within five minutes of the body becoming very tense as a result of stress and anxiety (Rathus and Nevid, 1977). The couple in this case illustration were taught some of the basic skills in a group session lasting three hours. They were then set a series of exercises to do in their own time which aimed to develop these basic skills and they then attended an 'advanced relaxation group' for a further two hours to refine and reinforce their mastery of relaxation.

Step 3 The helper worked carefully and sensitively in between the two group relaxation sessions on constructing a very detailed description of the behaviours John and Eileen engaged in when they had sex. This description was very detailed and included descriptions of foreplay, the language used to arouse Eileen by John and John by Eileen, the sequence the couple went through to the point of John's ejaculation and the after-sex behaviour of the couple. Whenever John or Eileen felt embarrassed, the helper encouraged them to use one of the 'quick' relaxation techniques they had learned in the first group session. On the basis of this behavioural analysis, the helper constructed a list of the actions which this couple engaged in, broken into 12 steps. Each step involved Eileen in progressively more anxiety – in other words, the list was a hierarchy of behaviours which Eileen found increasingly anxiety-laden. The list was agreed by both John and Eileen to be sequenced correctly and the helper was satisfied that his analysis of the sequence was suitable for the process to be followed.

Step 4 John and Eileen were asked to perform the first act on the list. In fact this was to engage in 'dirty talk'. They were to do this as they got into bed after a period of 10 minutes of relaxation. Whenever Eileen felt anxious they were to stop and go into a quick relaxation routine. During this phase of the process, the only form of sexual activity they were permitted by the helper to engage in was dirty talk. Whenever Eileen stopped the talk because she was feeling anxious and began to use the relaxation routine, she had been asked to imagine herself in a sauna with friends having a drink – a scene Eileen had reported to be the most relaxing she had experienced. At the end of four days, Eileen was able to cope with up to 40 minutes of 'dirty talk' and to engage fully in this talk herself without using the relaxation routine. The helper instructed the couple to repeat the same process for the next item on their structured hierarchy – caressing of Eileen's breasts by John. Again, Eileen was instructed to imagine her relaxing scene and to use the relaxation routine whenever she felt anxious. After three days, she was able to report feeling comfortable with John's caresses. The helper encouraged the couple to move on to the next item on their list and so the helping process continued until Eileen had achieved orgasm again after a helping period of 16 weeks.

This process is known as systematic desensitization because the helper encourages the couple to work systematically through a series of steps ordered from least anxiety-laden to most anxiety-laden using a method (relaxation) by which the body responses are desensitized.

This process, which involves the teaching of a skill (relaxation), the breaking up of behaviour into small and more manageable parts, the pairing of an established stimulus (e.g. dirty talk) with a new and learned response (relaxation) and the extinction of the old response through the use of imagination (the sauna scene) and behaviour (relaxation) are common features of a great many behavioural techniques. Indeed, these elements are commonplace in the work educational psychologists undertake with the parents of children with special needs (e.g. Raymond, 1984).

Systematic desensitization has been used in the treatment of anxiety and phobias, including agoraphobia (Bandura, 1969; Rachman, 1968). In addition it has been used for more complex behavioural problems, such as the tendency for a family to argue (see Rachman and Wilson, 1980). In this latter case the hierarchy of behaviours constructed by the helper was as follows:

1. Initiate a topic in which the family is known to disagree (e.g. the eldest son is thinking of joining the police force and the father objects; the mother supports and the younger brother gets violent). When the father speaks the discussion stops and relaxation commences by all family members. (The eldest son is responsible for initiating both the discussion and the relaxation.)
2. When this topic is next discussed, the relaxation occurs after each occasion at which the mother speaks. The mother is responsible for initiating the relaxation routine.
3. On a subsequent occasion when this topic occurs, relaxation occurs whenever either of the two sons makes any contribution (verbal or physical) and the father is responsible for initiating this process.

Whilst this is an unusual form of desensitization, it has been used to some effect in reducing family tension and encouraging better interpersonal communication within the family.

A common feature of all systematic desensitization programmes is the use of homework assignments by the helper. The individual or the members of the family with whom the helper is working are asked to perform tasks at home under specific conditions and to report on the consequences of performing these tasks when they next meet the helper. Indeed, a great many behavioural programmes are now available for self-administration by individuals and families (e.g. Rathus and Navid, 1977). For the helper to be able to ask a couple, a person or a family to undertake homework tasks or to disclose the specific and precise details of their sexual behaviour, as John and Eileen did, requires the helper to show a great deal of sensitivity, warmth and acceptance towards those he or she is helping. It also requires that the helper adjusts and redesigns the programme of desensitization to fit those with whom he or she is working.

Modelling

Systematic desensitization, as we have seen, is an operant conditioning technique in the sense in which Skinner uses the term. Modelling is a different technique which owes much more to the idea of behaviour shaping. The term 'modelling' here refers to the process by which a person, couple or family learns new behaviours by observing others perform these behaviours. The behaviours upon which helpers focus are behaviours which the client or family finds difficult or distressing to perform, but whose performance would in fact be helpful to them. Three kinds of modelling programmes have been developed (Rachman, 1976). The first involves the family or couple or individual watching someone in the same room they are in doing something which they would find distressing to do. This is referred to as *live modelling*. For example, imagine that Mr Williams is afraid of snakes. Live modelling would involve Mr Williams watching another person handling snakes in close proximity to himself. A second form of modelling is for the model to perform the behaviour on film or video. Our Mr Williams would then watch a model handle snakes on film. This is referred to as *symbolic modelling*. A final form of modelling is when the client is asked to imagine a model performing the behaviour they find distressing – our Mr Williams would be encouraged to imagine in detail someone handling snakes. This form of modelling is usually referred to as *covert modelling*.

The theory that lies behind this procedure is to reduce the anxiety associated with untried behaviours (anxiety has become the response to the stimulus of an untried behaviour) by 'disinhibiting' the client. That is to say, the client is provided with safe environments within which it is possible to experiment with the behaviour in question. Some brief case illustrations will make clear what this process involves.

Example 1 June and David Dale were expecting their first child in seven months and June was having nightmares about the birth. She always fainted at the sight of blood, had never been in hospital, feared the thought of being there and had never really experienced pain. June's anxiety over this coming event was upsetting David, so much so in fact that he was drinking heavily so that he could sleep through the nightmares that June was having.

The health visitor heard of June's anxiety and, working with a clinical psychologist, she arranged for June to watch in her own home at first a series of videos depicting various stages of actual labour. June was able to see women of her own age using 'gas and air' to reduce pain; able to see their husbands present throughout the birth; able to see the hospital facilities she would be using and able to listen to the comments of the 'models' after the birth. Nearer the expected birth date, June was taken by the health visitor and local midwife (who would be supporting June after her return home from birth) to the maternity unit and shown round. In particular, she was shown the rooms in which the first stages of labour took place and was able to meet several women in these early stages of their labour. She found the staff on duty to be very friendly and the women in labour she met did not seem to her to be going through the agony she had anticipated but were experiencing some 'discomfort'. One of the women (a 'model' for our purposes here) said that after two hours in labour it was no different from being on a continental bus tour, though she did expect the 'road' to get a bit bumpier as the journey continued.

This modelling activity encouraged June to feel less anxious prior to the event but, more significantly, provided her with a series of behavioural images which she was able to use when she began her labour and was admitted to hospital. This programme of activity also had a beneficial effect upon her relationship with David in the period leading up to the birth.

Example 2 Anne is the victim of an aggressive and battering husband. She has three children and is severely depressed by her situation. She wants to leave her husband and fears for the safety of herself and her children – her husband has become increasingly violent. However, she feels that she is unable to leave because she has no independent source of income and no friends that would look after her who would be able to protect her from her husband. She visits a local women's group.

The women's group spends some time with her, identifying the choice of fears that she faces – the fear of leaving and the fear of staying. They seek to establish a climate in which leaving is seen in a more positive light than staying. They then ask her to spend a day (unbeknown to her husband) at the refuge for battered women, just helping them with routine tasks (e.g. cooking, cleaning). There she meets a number of women who have been through the process she fears. Whilst she is there, a woman and two children arrive having left the family home only minutes before. She is able to witness the behaviour of this woman, who seems relieved to have made the decision, and the behaviour of the others at the refuge. She is able to notice the way in which other battered women at the centre support her and care for the children immediately, even though none of them had met this woman before. She is therefore provided with a model of the behaviour which she herself might subsequently (and in fact did) engage in.

We have interpreted the term 'modelling' in a more liberal sense than many behavioural helpers would like through these examples, though we feel that the examples highlight the potential of modelling for a variety of situations. Most commonly, modelling is used in relation to phobias (including agoraphobia) and anxiety, especially over-anxious parents (Windheuser, 1977). Symbolic modelling has also been used to help couples experiencing sexual difficulties which are seen to be anxiety related (e.g. premature ejaculation in men and orgasm failure in women). Modelling is used extensively in parent-effectiveness training programmes, such as those described by Gordon (1970).

Assertiveness Training

A specific form of modelling is referred to as assertiveness training. Many people confuse the idea of assertiveness with aggression. Before examining the nature of assertiveness it is necessary to establish clearly the difference between being assertive and being aggressive.

Aggression is usually some kind of expression which is inappropriate in intensity to the situation and it is usually achieved at someone else's expense; assertiveness involves emotional honesty, appropriate reactions to situations and a consideration of the needs and feelings of other people. Aggression is characterized by righteousness and superiority, whereas assertiveness is characterized by confidence and self-respect. People value and respect assertiveness whereas they feel humiliated and threatened by aggression. Assertiveness is used to establish a position; aggression is used to challenge. Although there is sometimes a fine line between aggression and assertivenesss, there is such a thing as responsible assertiveness which can be productive for the person who practises it and can lead to the resolution of conflict (Lange and Jakubowski, 1976).

In behavioural terms, assertiveness training is a procedure by which people who find themselves unable to cope with conflict or challenge and who lack self-confidence can be taught some particular communication skills which will help them behave confidently and communicate their own needs, thoughts and feelings more effectively. Assertiveness training is a special form of communication skills training and has been used in marital and family work. Here is a brief case example which illustrates the kind of work that is undertaken by helpers working with this technique. In this case the family was referred to the helper by an educational psychologist.

Example 1 Janet is 16 and is very shy and withdrawn. Her father pushes and presses her to be more confident – each time he pushes her she seems to retreat more and more into herself. Her mother, who is also lacking in confidence (though less so than Janet), tells her to ignore her father's pushy behaviour and to take her time to be what she wants to be and behave how she wants to behave. Janet tells the helper that she would like to behave more confidently and would like not to feel threatened in a group or family situation, but that she just does not know how to go about it. Being told to do it, she says, does not help her; she needs to be shown what to do.

The helper talks with the mother and father in Janet's absence for some time. He seeks to establish detailed descriptions of family situations in which Janet's behaviour has been a source of concern and to document the behaviours of both parents in such situations. He notices that whenever Janet does not behave in a way the father thinks she should (e.g. when faced with family friends asking her about her career intentions or when asked about her plans for summer) he becomes angry with her; also, whenever she attempts to behave in a more confident way the father shows no interest in her behaviour and does not appear to respond. The helper also notes that the father behaves in a similar way to his wife during the course of this assessment interview – a point returned to later.

The helper, working with the whole family, outlines a programme of skill training aimed at enhancing the quality of the family's communication pattern. The programme seeks to establish some principles about communication, to teach some specific communications skills and to practise these skills in role-play and real situations.

The first phase of the programme in which all family members participate concerns the principles which the family accept as a basis for communication. The listing given in Murgatroyd and Woolfe (1982, p. 153) is used as a starting point for this work. It includes statements such as 'We have the right to decide whether or not we will meet the expectations others have of us' and 'We have the right to change our minds' and 'We have the right to be silent' and 'We have the right to ask others to respond to our needs and to decide whether we respond to theirs'. Each item is discussed at length. The helper points out occasions during the course of this phase in which, even after agreeing on a particular statement, the father has behaved in a way contrary to this agreement. For each statement in the list which the family develops during this activity, the helper works with the family to develop a clear understanding of the behavioural implications of the statement. For example, if Janet does choose to exercise her right to remain silent, what behaviours might the mother and father need to use in order to show Janet that they respect her right to be silent? This detailed statement of principles linked to behaviour, elicited over three sessions, is presented at the fourth session in a typewritten form as a sort of written contract for the family. This procedure (known as contingency contracting and described more fully below) establishes some behavioural rules for the family as a whole which each of its members can refer to.

Following presentation of this 'contract', the helper begins to identify specific behaviours which the family can use to fulfil the aspirations represented in the contract. For example, the helper shows Janet (by modelling and role play) that she is able to say to her father, 'I am not sure about my career choice yet, but I can see that you want me to make some decision soon. I will talk to you about it from time to time and make a decision before long.' At the same time, the helper encourages the father to acknowledge Janet's need to take her time in making up her mind. A variety of specific communication skills are worked through amongst all family members, usually using role play in pairs. The helper uses Janet's behaviour within these sessions as a gauge for the progress the family is making; he also carefully observes changes in the behaviour of Janet's father, who shows less aggression and more tolerance as the sessions continue. After 10 sessions, the helper ends the programme of work, but agrees to contact the family after a month has gone by.

Follow-up a month after the skill training programme reveals that the father and mother have become more communicative both with each other and with Janet. Janet is still quiet, though she does volunteer comments far more than was the case prior to the programme. The helper sets the family a series of communication tasks to be completed within the next two months, after which another follow-up session will take place.

This case contains a variety of 'standard' behavioural helping process components: careful behavioural assessment, the identification of specific goals, the teaching of specific skills, careful observation and monitoring of progress, the use of homework tasks, and a concern to evaluate the impact of the programme. Though some time is invested in this family by the helper, positive results do appear to be beginning to emerge. From the perspective of family focused helping, the case also illustrates the use of pairs within the family (mother–daughter, daughter–father, father–mother) through role play – suggesting that this behavioural programme adopts the view suggested by Patterson and Reid (1970), namely that the family is viewed by this helper as a collection of interlocking and mutually dependent pairs.

This programme of assertiveness is just one of several possible programmes. Many more have been described in the literature (see, for example, Carmody, 1978) and helpers may find themselves devising their own programmes to suit the particular circumstances with which they find themselves presented. In so doing, it may be useful to bear in mind that family focused assertiveness is useful primarily in three situations: (a) in helping a family member to stand up for him- or herself within or beyond the family when he or she feels unjustly treated; (b) in enabling a family member to respond more directly to those events in his or her life which have significant consequences for him or her; and (c) in helping a family member to express love and affection towards some significant person in his or her life. Assertiveness is a major vehicle for reducing fear associated with communication of needs, thoughts and feelings and has a long history of development within behaviourism.

Contingency Contracting

In the last case illustration, use was made of contracting to some extent: the family members were asked to agree to respect the rights of each other and the behaviours that accompanied these rights. But it was a weak form of contracting. In the more developed forms, to be described here, systematic reinforcements are given to the performance of specific tasks documented in the contract and the contract itself is far more specific. Let us again illustrate the ideas behind this form of helping with a case illustration, adapted from the work of Liberman and Roberts (1976).

Example 1 Sarah is a 30-year-old married ex-secretary with three children. She requests help for what she describes as depression and marital disharmony. The helpers describe her as looking at least 10 years older than her actual age – very tired and haggard. A social work report makes clear that Sarah's depression involves a complete loss of interest in anything: she stays in bed for long periods of time and she is unable to cope with housework and the care of her three children. The social worker reports that Sarah feels she 'is a nothing' and suggests that 'the husband colludes with this by showing no emotion or affect [*sic*] with her'.

The first stage of the helping process with Sarah and her husband (the children are not directly involved in this process) involves a detailed behavioural analysis aimed at identifying what the behavioural problems are, how they have arisen in terms of the history of stimulus–response–reinforcement patterns and how they are now sustained. As a result of this stage of work (which lasted two weeks) the helpers identify five specific behavioural problems and suggest and agree with the couple the treatment goals that they are to pursue. Table 3 summarizes these problems and goals, and in doing so makes very clear just how specific the behavioural analysis has been.

Table 3 'Problems' and 'goals' resulting from a behavioural analysis of Sarah's situation (from Liberman and Roberts, 1976, p. 21)

	Problems	Goals
	Deficits	*Behaviour to strengthen*
1	Fails to perform housework and child care	Cleaning, clothes washing, making beds, going shopping, cooking meals, making snacks for children
2	Poor grooming	Fix hair more stylishly, wear more colourful clothes, iron clothes so they are not baggy or wrinkled
3	Infrequent conversation with husband and children	At least 15 minutes of conversing with husband each day, reading to children in evening
	Excesses	*Behaviour to decrease*
1	Complaints about helplessness and worthlessness	Verbalizations about feeling sick, helpless, worthless, 'like a nothing'
2	Retreating to bed	Time spent in bed during daytime and before 11 p.m. each evening

Once the couple had agreed that this listing was a statement of the behavioural features of their problem, the helpers then assisted the couple in negotiating a contingency contract. As can be seen from this contract, presented in summary in Table 4, Sarah's behaviour is made *contingent* upon her husband's behaviour; it is therefore the case that her husband's behaviour is contingent upon hers. Notice in this contract just how specific the behavioural contract is.

Table 4 An elementary contingency contract for Sarah and her husband Jack (from Liberman and Roberts, 1976, p. 216)

Sarah's responsibilities	Jack's responsibilities
Contract I	
Sit and talk with husband during breakfast, Monday to Friday	Arise from bed by 10 a.m. on Saturday and Sunday
Clean the living room for two hours each week	Engage in some mutual activity with wife between 10 and 11 p.m. on Tuesday, Thursday, Saturday and Sunday
Contract II Same as above plus the following:	
Dress in clothes that appeal to husband	Arrive at home by 5.30 p.m. each day
Initiate affection (kisses, hugs, hand holding, caresses) toward husband	Avoid expressing hostility or 'uptightness' (coldness, rejection, annoyance, silence, withdrawal) when wife asks not to pursue sexual relations

Having agreed this contract the couple were then instructed that, whenever one partner met some feature of this contract (e.g. whenever Sarah cleaned the living room for two hours in a week) the other partner was to issue a written receipt which was used to symbolize the recognition by one partner that the other was making progress. At the same time as this homework task was being performed, the helper coached the couple in communication skills, especially those associated with the communication of affection and concern.

Liberman and Roberts (1976), the helpers in this case, report that as satisfactory progress was being made (involving the resumption of intercourse), the contingency contract was extended and elaborated and covered increasingly complex communication skills.

This case, in our view, adequately presents the nature of contingency contracting. It makes explicit the idea that reinforcements (in this case in the form of receipts) are awarded when a feature of the contract is fulfilled and an additional contingent reinforcement occurs when the behaviour of one partner is rewarded by the agreed reciprocal behaviour of the other.

Contingency contracting is especially useful in three kinds of family situation: (a) to help a family member initiate specific actions which he or she finds anxiety-provoking; (b) to establish some clear-cut criteria for achievement so that a family member can 'know where they stand' in relation either to some goal or to another family member; and (c) when one family member wishes the consequences of his or her behaviour to be explicit in terms of the behaviour he or she observes from other family members.

Behavioural contracts usually involve seven basic elements:

(a) There should be a clear and detailed description of the behaviour(s) the person is being asked to perform.
(b) Some time limit should be set on the duration of behaviour. In our example, Jack is asked to engage in mutual activity for a specific time period and Sarah is asked to engage in cleaning work in the home for a specific period of time each week.
(c) The contract should specify the nature of the reinforcements. In our example, Sarah was reinforced each time she performed a behaviour either by a receipt or by reciprocal behaviour from Jack or by both these forms of reinforcement.
(d) Provision should be made for some aversive consequence if contracts are not fulfilled. In our example no clear aversive agreement existed.
(e) A 'bonus' clause might be included to indicate additional reinforcements for the person who exceeds the minimum terms of the contract.
(f) A specific way of recording the performance of the person in terms of the contract needs to be established at the outset. In the example the receipts, in addition to acting as a token reinforcer, also provided a way of recording compliance with the contract.
(g) The helper should seek to ensure that reinforcements follow as quickly as possible upon the performance of the behaviour so as to provide (as nearly as possible) immediate positive reinforcements for compliance with the contract.

Whilst these seven features may not always be present, they are basic features which helpers should bear in mind if they are considering using contingency contracts in marital and family work (Jacobson, 1977).

Problem-solving

Before describing the behavioural approach to problem-solving, it is important to differentiate this approach from that envisaged and described by Jay Hayley in his text *Problem-solving Therapy – New Strategies for Effective Family Therapy* (Hayley, 1976). Whilst the approach outlined by Hayley has behavioural components (most notably the setting of tasks and the insistence that the tasks are performed as a condition of helping), it is not exclusively behavioural and involves a number of strategic and structural features aimed at changing the communication structure of the family using some of the techniques described in Chapter 3 of the present text. Hayley's methods as described in his book are of considerable interest to the family focused helper, but they are best thought of as an outcome of the communications approach to helping (see Chapter 3) rather than the behavioural approach.

This observation, it is useful to note, reinforces the point made earlier in this book, namely that helping is much more of a pragmatic activity than the theoretical distinctions between the schools of helping might suggest – Jay Hayley is a ubiquitous master of pragmatism.

From a behavioural perspective, problem-solving is a helping process which aims to help a family deal more effectively with a wide range of situational problems. Although the use of problem-solving begins with a particular issue, the helper's task is to promote a generalized skill of problem-solving which the family can use in other situations without the helper's intervention. To do so, the helper will need to develop a climate of trust and understanding – a point we continually emphasize – and to conduct helping only after a period of behavioural analysis. Although the teaching of problem-solving skills has many educational features, the helper needs to remain sensitive to the reactions of those with whom he or she is working and needs to monitor carefully the way in which each family member reacts to the tasks in hand. Though we present case illustrations here which involve several family members, the processes we outline can be used equally effectively with individuals.

D'Zurilla and Goldfried (1971) outline a five-step approach to the problem-solving process. The five steps are as follows:

1 *General orientation* – setting the framework within which the family thinks about its problems
2 *Problem definition and formulation* – crystallizing the way in which a family conceptualizes its problems

3 *Generation of alternatives* – using brainstorming and other methods to identify a range of possible responses to a problem
4 *Decision making* – choosing between the alternatives generated at stage 3
5 *Verification* – evaluation of the consequences of the decision, monitoring effects and reviewing options.

We offer a brief description of each of these processes below and illustrate them by reference to work with families affected by unemployment or the threat of unemployment.

At the first stage the helper needs to encourage the family members to think not so much about the specific problem they have encountered but about their attitudes to problems in general. Helpers at this stage have four specific tasks. The first is to encourage the family to regard problems as a normative feature of family life – problems are a normal occurrence in families and families who experience them need not feel 'victimized' or unusual. This seems obvious when written down in this way, but it is not always so clear when a problem arises. For example, when the authors have worked with families affected by unemployment it has been a common experience that families ask 'what will others think about us'. This question is asked in small communities where three out of four families are affected by unemployment and in a country with at least three million unemployed – the family members still think that their problem experience marks them out and makes them special victims in some way. A similar feature of family thinking is that problems should not occur. Whilst it can be argued that unemployment should not occur on the scale that it does, it cannot be argued that problems of substance should not arise in families. The helper's task is to encourage the recognition of the normality of life being problematic. One way in which this can be achieved is to encourage the family members to recognize past situations which they saw at the time as problematic but which they subsequently coped with – examples include the birth of children or the death of a close relative. The helper uses such examples to highlight the fact that problems can be coped with. The next task the helper has at this stage is to encourage the family members to consider the ways in which they identify for themselves the fact that a problem is occurring. With unemployment it is reasonably clear cut. But other problems, such as the onset of some serious illness, can 'creep up' on a family and suddenly confront its members. The helper needs to help the family members look critically at their skills of problem recognition. Finally, the helper needs to encourage the family not to act impulsively when faced with a problem but to think through the various stages of problem-solving. In the case of some unemployed families, they have sold their existing houses and moved to another area where they think work might be more available, only to find themselves in a similar situation in a strange location. Acting impulsively in this way is a way of coping, but it is a way that adds to rather than reduces a problem.

In all this work, the helper needs to be sensitive to the predicament of the family and show high levels of empathy and genuineness. A failure to communicate these elements of the helping process will lead the family to believe that the helper is just 'treating' them as another case. This applies to each of the stages documented below.

The second stage is more directly concerned with the specific problem the family has presented. The task is essentially concerned with translating abstract feelings of 'having a problem' to concrete statements about the problem itself. One common difficulty in working with families is that the family produces lists of facts. In the case of the Statham family, affected by the father's unexpected unemployment, the family produced an itemized budget statement (including the costs of each child's underwear), a detailed description of all their valuables which they were willing to sell through a local newspaper, a list of all the jobs that appeared in the local newspaper that the father had applied for, a list of all the part-time jobs the mother had applied for and a costing of the relative merits of their son going to university (he already had been offered a place), being unemployed and receiving benefit payments or joining a government training scheme. The family had lost themselves in a mass of concrete facts and had lost sight of the issues these facts represented. The helper's task, working with the family, was to identify concrete *issues* that the family now needed to work on. In this case these were: (a) maximizing income whilst minimizing expenditure; (b) securing the future well-being of their children; (c) making good use of time; (d) not being pushed into actions which the family members, as a family, had not carefully considered; and (e) retaining the self-respect of the individual family members. Whilst these issues were reflected in the facts that the Statham family were amassing, the sharpness of these issues was getting lost in the detail they were accumulating.

The third stage is the generation of alternatives. Brainstorming is most commonly used at this stage. This is a process in which all family members are involved. Taking each issue at a time, the helper asks the family (a) to generate as many possible solutions to the problem as they can imagine – quantity being more important than quality; (b) in thinking about the ways of overcoming problems, to defer judgement about the quality of the idea until later – all ideas have value. The motto we have found useful as helpers at this stage is 'quantity breeds quality'. In the case of the Statham family one brainstorming activity focused on the question 'What should Father do with his £2300 redundancy money?' The family had originally intended to use it to pay off bills and debts until Father found a job. In a brainstorming session a great many ideas (54 in all) were generated. These included: (a) 'Put it all on a horse and pray' (suggested by Andrew, aged 10); (b) 'Use it to start a business – window cleaning or something' (Father); (c) 'Invest it and use the interest for our expenses' (Mother); (d) 'Use it to place an advert in the press advertising your availability for work' (John, 18 years); and (e) 'Pay off a chunk of the mortgage' (Mother). The helper encouraged the family to accept at this stage any suggestion, no matter how bizarre or amusing, since it is often the case that the humour of one suggestion triggers a new idea in someone else's mind. In addition to generating a large range of alternatives, this process is a way of building some communality in the family, especially if all of them have been involved in the task.

The next stage is to engage in the decision-making process. Here the helper works with the family to estimate which of the alternatives generated at the previous stage are worth pursuing. Some of the suggestions can usually be excluded quickly (e.g. Andrew's betting option in the last example) but others will need to be examined in terms of the likely consequences, given the issues identified at stage 2. At this stage helpers should encourage the family to think of four different kinds of consequence: (a) *personal consequences*, particularly as they relate to the major issues identified; (b) *social consequences*, especially the impact that a particular course of action would have on other family members; (c) *short-term consequences* in terms of the issues identified and other family members; and (d) *longer-term consequences* for the family and for future problem experiences of the family. In our experience, families faced with problems confuse these different kinds of consequence and find it difficult to reach a decision in a rational way. It is also our experience that families continue to look for an ideal solution, even though many problems which families experience have no ideal solution. Situations involving a major financial crisis, terminal illness, death of a family member or some major unexpected crisis have no satisfactory solution. The task of decision making is to make the best choice given the available options. Once the family members reach a decision about the option they wish to pursue it is then necessary to explore the precise way in which this option is to be pursued. For example, the Statham family decided to experiment with the idea of running a small family business (an option that was not in their minds when they first sought help). The helper worked with the family once they had made this decision, aiding them in identifying what kind of business and how they might go about establishing it. The helper involved others at this stage too (e.g. the Co-operative Development Agency, the Manpower Services Commission, the Small Firms Unit, etc.).

The final phase of the decision-making process is verification. Essentially this stage involves the family members in evaluating the consequences of the action they actually embark upon in terms of the issues raised at stage 2. That is, after the family has implemented the decision of its members, the helper encourages the family to review the actual consequences of working in the way the family has chosen. In the case of the Statham family, the helper worked with the family members for three months (one hour per week) after the decision to start their own business was taken. In this time he helped the family members to look at: (a) the consequences of their decision for the family's finances; (b) the impact the decision had had upon their feelings of self-respect and on the relationships within the family; (c) the way in which this decision had had an impact on the future well-being of the children. In addition, the helper reinforced the value of the decision-making process which the family had worked through as a way of dealing with difficult problems.

Although the illustration here concerns the problem of unemployment, this process has been used in a variety of problem situations, including drug abuse and addiction (Copermann, 1973), crisis situations (McGuire and Sifnoes, 1970), and conflict in the family – especially that focused around children (Spivack and Shure, 1974). Whilst we have presented problem-solving here as a helping process in its own right (which it is), it is most commonly used as an adjunct to some other behavioural method, such as contingency contracting, assertiveness training or modelling. One other point also needs to be made about the presentation of this (and other) methods in this chapter. We have outlined the logical structure of the helping process. In reality, the use of this process is less precise than is indicated here and involves the helper making sensitive judgements about the family and its members. Helpers should not treat the stages outlined briefly here as if they were a 'cook book' approach to helping. Rather, the stages as outlined indicate some of the features of this complex helping process.

Communication Skills Training

As the term implies, this form of helping aims to teach a person or a couple or a family the skills of effective communication. In particular, the behaviourally oriented helper seeks to maximize the 'goodness of fit' between that which the person intends to communicate and that which the person actually communicates. That is to say, the methods used in communication skills training are intended to reduce incongruity and to increase the directness of a person's communications.

A great many social skills training programmes or parent skills programmes are essentially communication skills programmes. For example, Thomas Gordon's *Parent Effectiveness Training* (Gordon, 1970) seeks to promote the behavioural skills of listening attentively, giving feedback to the children and the marriage partner to show that they have been heard, matching verbal and nonverbal behaviours and using statements which clearly express intention. More specific programmes, such as those developed by O'Leary and Turkewitz (1978), seek to promote effective communication in the face of marital conflict by making extensive use of video replay facilities, behavioural shaping and modelling activity.

Assertiveness training, described briefly above, is a specific form of communication skills training. For in assertiveness, the person is encouraged to communicate effectively and without aggression his or her thoughts and feelings to other family members. The case example used in that section conveys the essential elements of the process of helping used in communication skills training and will not be duplicated here. The point to note is that this method, normally used as an adjunct to other helping processes, aims to affect the communication behaviours (tone of voice, body posture, eye movement, phrases used) of a particular family member who has difficulty communicating with another family member. This behavioural approach has been used extensively with children and in marital relationships (see the training programme by Becvar, 1974).

Cognitive Behaviour Therapy

The discerning reader will have noted that not all of the helping processes outlined in this chapter are concerned with specific behaviours. For example, problem-solving aims at promoting a generic set of behavioural skills which are broadly defined to specific situations. Other processes, such as assertiveness training, are concerned with affecting both the way a person thinks (cognition) and the way that he or she behaves. Cognitive behaviour therapy seeks to affect behaviour through reframing and modifying the way in which a person thinks.

The rationale for this approach has two sources. The first is the research work by a variety of behaviourally oriented workers which has examined the relationship between the way in which a person evaluates or labels his or her situation and his or her emotional and behavioural reactions to such situations. For example, is a person who labels a forthcoming examination as 'an intellectual snake pit' more likely to experience pre-exam nerves than the person who labels this same exam as 'a natural way of ending any advanced course of study'? Research gives strong evidence in support of the view that the statements with which an individual provides him- or herself about a situation do indeed have implications for subsequent emotional and behavioural reactions (May, 1977; Rogers and Craighead, 1977).

The second source for this form of helping has been the work of Albert Ellis, a leading American psychotherapist who has influenced several therapists in Britain (e.g. Dryden, 1984). Ellis observed, 'If . . . people become disturbed because they unthinkingly accept certain illogical premises or irrational ideas, then there is good reason to believe that they can be somehow persuaded or taught to think more logically and rationally and thereby undermine their own disturbances' (Ellis, 1962).

Central to the helping process suggested by Ellis is the suggestion that there are certain irrational beliefs, expectations or assumptions which individuals and families use when they consider their situation and find that they are experiencing distress. In the context of family life, these typical irrational beliefs can be summarized as follows: (a) the idea that it is essential to be shown love and approval at all times by all family members; (b) the idea that it would be awful or terrible if one was thought not to be achieving or adequate by other members of the family; (c) the idea that if one is bad or wicked the family will always find it necessary to respond with punishment and harm; (d) the idea that it is awful or catastrophic when things do not go the way either the family or oneself thinks that they should; (e) the idea that unhappiness or distress within a family is always caused by some external force and that this implies that there is nothing a family can do to control its members' sorrows and disturbances; (f) the idea that if something has the potential for being distressing or dangerous all members of the family should show equal concern for it and should constantly worry about the consequence of this 'something' occurring; (g) the idea that it is easier to avoid an issue that affects the family rather than to face that issue with the family; (h) the idea that the family will always need a strong outsider to help it with its problems, since it would not be able to handle its problems without such help; (i) the idea that the family's past history will always determine the present, such that if there was a failure at something in the past the family will fail if it attempts this something again in the future; (j) the idea that other family members have to be upset if one member experiences some difficulty or distress – a failure to do so would weaken one's position in the family; (k) the idea that there is an invariable right, correct, perfect and obvious solution to all family problems and that it will be catastrophic if this solution cannot be found.

If a family experiences distress, Ellis suggests, one or more of these irrational beliefs may be a part of its members' thinking processes and may in fact be regarded as a cause of the distress. For example, the idea that there is a perfect solution to all problems (irrational belief (k)) may prevent a family from responding to some situation which its members are experiencing since they do not feel that the solutions they are contemplating are 'perfect enough'; this irrational belief thus inhibits action and is likely to create its own distress. To affect the level of distress in such a family, the helper will need to change this irrational belief in some way.

There are a variety of ways in which the helper can tackle the task of changing a family's thinking processes once its members have recognized that it is thinking that is contributing to the level of distress in the family. The choice the helper makes of method will depend upon his or her familiarity with the process, the nature of the problem presented by the family, the motivation of the family to change and the extent to which the helper is confident that it is the thinking and belief system of the family that is perpetuating the distress. Meichenbaum (1977) discusses several different forms of helping along these lines in an especially clear and instructive way. Here we concentrate on the four stages of the helping process associated with *rational restructuring*.

The first stage of the helping process which aims to change the way a family thinks about its situation involves the helper in explaining the underlying assumptions of rational restructuring. These are: (a) that what we 'tell ourselves' about a situation becomes what we believe about that situation – for example, if we believe that it is hopeless for us to try something then generally we do not attempt that activity; (b) that we are very sophisticated in the way in which we hear these messages – we do not literally speak to ourselves (though sometimes this does happen) but rather we find ourselves acting as if we had spoken to ourselves along the lines of one or more of the irrational beliefs listed here. The aim here is that the helper should establish, in the minds of those family members involved, the idea that the way in which they are thinking creates their distress. An abundance of examples is necessary if the helper is to be effective in making this point.

In the next stage, the helper seeks to move from establishing the general principle to the specific situation the family is facing. The helper, working closely with the family, seeks to identify which of the 11 irrational beliefs (a)–(k) are associated with the specific situation which the family is presenting. In our experience, it is useful to present beliefs in extreme forms so that the family disagrees with them. This is precisely what the helper is aiming to achieve – the rejection of irrational beliefs. When the family hesitates over some belief, the helper needs to focus upon this belief most carefully. He or she needs to emphasize the difference between thinking 'Wouldn't it be nice if . . .?' and thinking 'It is essential . . .' or 'We must . . .' or 'We should . . .'; this distinction is concerned with establishing the extent to which a particular idea is an imperative for action (a should or a must) versus being a desired but not essential end point. The primary goal which the helper pursues at this stage is encouragement of the family to agree that certain of the beliefs upon which it has been acting are unrealistic and to identify a number of very specific reasons for such beliefs being so regarded.

In the third stage of this process, helpers need to encourage the family members to recognize the precise way in which their holding of an irrational belief has had consequences both for the way they behave and for the way in which they feel. This involves the helper actively exploring the emotional and behavioural features of the distress the family has presented and linking these features back to the holding of the irrational belief. Often during this process further irrational beliefs come to light and it will be necessary for the helper to work on these newly observed irrational beliefs in the way reported at stage 2. The aim throughout this stage is to encourage the family members most involved in maintaining the irrational belief that they are the cause of their own distress and that they want to change the way they are thinking so that their distress can be reduced.

As an illustration, consider the wife who has become upset that her husband no longer takes her out dancing – something they used to do when they were first married. The husband gives three reasons for not going dancing: (a) they have three children and the costs of baby-sitting make an evening out very expensive; (b) since they married he has been promoted several times at work and is now extremely tired on return from work; (c) when he is home he likes to spend his time with the family as a whole and is not particularly interested in going out – he already feels he is away from the family too much. His wife reacts to this by thinking that 'because he doesn't take me dancing he doesn't love me any more'. She reacts to this in extreme ways and they have started to argue more than ever before, so much so that it is beginning to be noticed by their children. The helper helps the couple to identify that their difficulty is not whether or not they go dancing, but rather it is the wife's thought that 'it is essential to be shown love and approval at all times' (irrational belief (a)) that is the source of the distress. When recognized in this way, it becomes possible for both partners to see their difficulty in a new way. The helper has then to explore with this couple alternative versions of this belief which are more rational. For example, the family explores the helper's suggestion that 'it would be really nice if each of us could show love and affection at all times to all other members of the family, but it will not be awful or terrible if, from time to time, this does not happen'. The helper works hard at encouraging a different message for the wife, whilst at the same time encouraging the husband to modify the way he reacts to his wife's requests to have some entertainment.

The basic process of rational restructuring is outlined in this example: the helper seeks to identify the irrational belief that is behind the distress and then seeks to change it by first disputing the irrational belief and then helping the family to identify and use a more rational belief. This last step – changing the beliefs held – is the final stage of this helping process. The task is a difficult one: the helper has to encourage rational thinking whilst the family is in the situation – thinking rationally with hindsight is not an effective way of reducing distress. In this stage considerable use is made of what is termed 'rational–emotive imagery' (Dryden, 1984). This is a technical term for something rather simple: the helper encourages the family members to imagine that they are in the situation which they find distressing and then encourages them to rehearse their responses using rational belief rather than the irrational belief they have identified. Alternatively, role play can be used to encourage the family to practise the behaviours that accompany the new rational belief. A final step here is for the helper to offer incomplete sentences for family members to complete. For example, if the family is seeking to deal with a different issue concerning one of their children, called Mike, the helper might offer the following incomplete sentences: (a) 'I/We will still love Mike even if . . . .' (b) 'Though we might be upset if Mike continues to behave in this way, we recognize that his behaviour need not make us feel . . . .' (c) 'Mike has presented us with a problem; though there is no perfect solution we . . . .' The purpose of these incomplete sentences is to encourage the family to recognize the behavioural and interpersonal implications of a rational approach to their situation.

Although we have presented this helping process as a four-stage process, our experience is that these stages run into each other and can become very involved. Also, the stage at which the helper seeks to change the belief system of a person or a family is an extremely difficult one – the helper has to dispute, challenge and confront an irrational belief, since families and individuals seek to cling to these beliefs with grim determination. The helper has to be hard on the family and look at the extreme consequences of maintaining this belief if the family is to be encouraged to abandon it. The process is therefore a powerful one and needs, if it is to be successful, to be based upon a trusting and genuine relationship between the helper and the family.

The Idea of 'Family Life Skills'

A number of the processes we have outlined in this chapter have been concerned with the helper acting as teacher to the family or to specific members of the family. For example, assertiveness training involves the helper teaching a family member or a family to be more direct and genuine in communications. Problem-solving is a process by which a family is taught, as a general skill, a way of coping with stressful or difficult problems. Rational restructuring is a way of teaching the family to think in such a way as to reduce distress rather than increase it. These examples suggest that the behavioural approach to helping, as outlined here, is as much about education as it is about handling personal and family distress.

Indeed, this idea is formalized in some of the writings about these methods which describe them as 'psycho-education', implying that the helper is seeking to educate the family and its members in basic psychological processes. Some authors, such as Hopson and Scally (1981), take this further and describe these kinds of skill teaching activities as 'life skills', suggesting that the helper is seeking to equip the person or the family with social and personal skills which are helpful in the task of living in the social world. In recent discussions with behavioural workers, the term 'family life skills' training has started to be applied to the kinds of processes we have outlined here. Thus behavioural approaches which are intended to have general as well as specific outcomes are seen in this much broader context of family life skills. Some recent writing has suggested that helpers, rather than waiting for families to experience distress before offering their help, might in fact regard 'family life skills' programmes as something worth offering to families as a basic educational activity through adult education centres, family networks and other logical organizations. Indeed, some of the materials produced by the Open University (e.g. *Parents and Teenagers*) already make use of some of the ideas and procedures outlined here. We mention this educational role for helpers as a way of pointing out that the choice between working with individuals, families or communities is appropriate here. One way of working with the community is to offer 'family life skills' education programmes.

Conclusion

This chapter has presented a great deal of information in a relatively short space about a number of different behavioural approaches to helping. The reader should not be seduced into thinking that this is a manual of behavioural procedures or that any one description is complete. A careful reading of *The Handbook of Behavioural Interventions – A Clinical Guide* (Goldstein and Foa, 1980) will reveal a variety of subtleties and processes which make these processes more complex. None the less, we have been able to present a full flavour of the behavioural approaches now used with families and couples seeking help.

Jones (1980) makes a very important point about these methods, which we reproduce here in full:

> 'Orientation to behavioural techniques is considered to be experimental and when a patient does not respond, the therapist uses an empirical attitude to ask "why"; for example, the steps in reinforcement might be too large, timing of reinforcement might be incorrect, or the overall behavioural plan might not fit the behaviour. The "patient is always right" and the burden is on the therapist to devise effective interventions. Such an approach may be contrasted to other family therapy approaches, where the tendency has been for the therapist to decide that failures are caused by patients who are inappropriate for techniques, rather than viewing the techniques as needing modification for a particular patient or family'.

One of the major contributions of the behavioural approach is to promote this experimental view of the helping process: the task is to find the best possible fit between the family, the helper and the helping process.

In this context, readers might find a comment by Whittaker (1976) helpful. He says, 'My theory is that all theories are bad except for the beginner's game playing, until he gets the courage to give up theories and just live.' By this he means that helping is a process of continual adjustment, refinement and testing. Adherence to one school at the expense of some process that might just be appropriate for a family is inappropriate for helpers engaged in family focused work.

In this chapter we have sought, as simply as possible, to present modern behavioural approaches. Not all behavioural approaches will find acceptance with helpers – there are some processes not described here which we would find difficult to use as part of our own repertoire of helping skills (e.g. aversion therapy). Counsellors and helpers who are unfamiliar with the behavioural approach may have been surprised by how humanistic many of the approaches we have outlined here actually are. Indeed, our hope is that this chapter has contributed in some small way to showing helpers how much they might already have in common with the behavioural approach.

6

THE ROLE OF A HELPER IN A FAMILY CRISIS

Introduction

Earlier chapters have examined the ways in which helpers might choose to work with individuals or subgroups of families or whole families in a family focused way. We have emphasized the importance of the helper consciously deciding on his or her orientation in approaching a given helping situation. Implicit in much of the materials presented so far is the assumption that the family has time to work through the helping processes we have described. For example, some of the case illustrations have taken several weeks and months. This chapter concerns a different type of problem which helpers face: the family member or family in crisis.

As we pointed out in an earlier book *Coping with Crisis – Understanding and Helping People in Need* (Murgatroyd and Woolfe, 1982), the term 'crisis' is best understood as a subjective and not an objective phenomenon. An event, such as becoming unemployed or having a daughter become pregnant though unmarried, may be perceived as a crisis by one family but as a hiccup or a nonproblem by another family. It is equally common for such events to be seen as a crisis by some family members but not by others. It follows, therefore, that an event only becomes a crisis if a person or family experiences it as such. Since a person or family may interpret a variety of events as crisis laden, it is not possible to describe 'typical' crisis events, though some situations (such as rape, terminal illness, death of a close relative, disfigurement through accident) do commonly and not surprisingly produce crisis reactions.

The feeling of being in crisis has a number of features. These include the following: (a) the individual or family feels threatened in some way, so much so that they feel that their identity as a person or family is being challenged; (b) they feel that their normal tried and tested ways of coping with situations are failing and as a result feel helpless and despondent; (c) because their normal coping strategies appear ineffective, they feel that they are unable to affect their situation no matter what actions they take and they therefore feel 'trapped' in their situation; finally (d) because the feelings of helplessness and despondency are coupled with the feeling of being trapped, all actions which they contemplate as ways of dealing with their crisis appear to involve tremendous risk, both to themselves and others – this feeling of risk further adds to their inability to take positive action.

These sets of responses to a situation amount to a crisis experience. Such experiences can arise in families in response to a myriad of things and helpers will be familiar with a variety of situations which produce such responses. For example, the relationship between a couple may break down because one partner discovers that the other has a lover; the birth of a baby may exacerbate underlying tensions within a family; the way in which an adolescent member of the family is growing and changing may create feelings of crisis in one or both parents and affect other members of the family; the loss of a job or the onset of some illness or the process of ageing may also be triggers for crisis experiences.

In this chapter we seek to explore more fully the meaning of crisis for a family, the potential such crises holds for change and the role which helpers can play in helping family members deal with crisis. In doing so we begin by acknowledging that crisis work is difficult for helpers – they have a short time in which to make some impact on the family's coping behaviour and do so under pressure. This creates special demands upon helpers which we have explored more fully elsewhere (Murgatroyd and Woolfe, 1982; Murgatroyd, 1983). Here our concern, as in the other chapters, is to present a framework within which helpers can work in a family focused way with individuals, subgroups or families who are experiencing a crisis.

Coping

One important construct we need to establish and define at the beginning of this chapter is that of 'coping'. Here we use this term not to describe whether or not a particular action is successful, but rather to describe a process. This is different from the common use of the term 'coping' as meaning an end product of some activity – e.g. 'He's coping better now that he's stopped smoking'. In our sense, coping is the group of processes which the person or family uses in attempting to resolve a crisis: coping may be successful or unsuccessful. A further difference between our conception of coping and that found in common speech is that we imply more than a behavioural action. Coping, in our sense, involves all the attempts made by a person or family to improve the quality of the 'fit' between themselves and their environment. It therefore involves understanding the way the person thinks, feels and behaves. A helper concerned with a person or family in crisis therefore needs to attend to the ways in which thinking, feeling and behaviour have shaped the crisis experience. For coping is not just a response to a crisis situation, it is also a shaper of that situation. Two examples illustrate clearly this last point.

Example 1 Mr and Mrs Turner have been married for four and a half years. They have one child, aged three. For some time their marital relationships have been undergoing significant stress and strain. Mr Turner copes with this by leaving the house early for work, arriving home late from work and spending his weekends fishing and golfing. That is, he minimizes his contact with the family so as to reduce the frequency with which he experiences stress in his contacts with his wife.

Mr Turner's coping strategy has the effect of increasing the stress Mrs Turner feels in her marriage. She complains of never seeing him, of him being off-hand when she does and of not being able to talk to him. Mr Turner's coping strategy actually precipitates the crisis in this family.

Example 2 Mr and Mrs Dee had been married for seven years when they became the parents of a physically handicapped son. Mr Dee was unable to accept this child and felt a great deal of hostility towards him. His response to the child was to distance himself from the child emotionally and physically – he rarely played with the child, rarely discussed the child with others and sought to minimize his physical contact with the child by not engaging in bathing, feeding and dressing him. The result for Mr Dee was that, in the short term at least, this form of coping brought benefits – it protected him from feeling overwhelmed about the implications of being the father of a handicapped child and from his feelings of loss and grief over the normal child he felt he should have had.

However, in distancing himself from his son he also distanced himself from his wife. As the years passed by, the continuance of this coping strategy meant that Mrs Dee saw herself as having to act increasingly as the buffer between her son and her husband. In fact, on a great many occasions she found herself having to choose between the needs being expressed to her by her son and the needs being expressed to her by her husband.

The coping strategy adopted by Mr Dee, though productive in one sense for some time, led in the long term to Mrs Dee having to choose who to live with: her husband or her son. She chose the son, whose needs were paramount to her. The husband's distancing was now complete. He was distanced from both his wife and his son.

These examples highlight the point that coping is a process and may not always be successful. Indeed, these examples highlight the differences between what might be described as 'intentions' and 'consequences' – Mr Dee and Mr Turner did not intend their coping actions to have the consequences which they had for their marriages. Their problems, from the helper's viewpoint, lay in their lack of know-how in translating intentions into action.

The Experience of Crisis in a Family

At the beginning of this chapter we outlined some features of the experience of crisis which we have found helpful in working with individuals and families. We have also found the listing of other features provided by Puryear (1975) helpful in identifying some of the related features of the experience of crisis which helpers find themselves faced with. These five features are as follows:

1 *Symptoms of stress*   These may be psychological, such as depression, anxiety, and irrational or obsessive thoughts, or they may be physical, such as headaches, illness, stomach pains, nausea and back-pain.
2 *Attitudes of panic or defeat*   The person or family feels that they have tried everything and there is nothing they can now do (defeat) or that they must frantically try anything anyone suggests since anything will be better than that which they are now experiencing (panic).

This leads to contradictory feelings of apathy or agitation and individuals and families often switch rapidly between these two feelings in a crisis.

3 *Focus on relief* The person or family focus their energies on the immediate relief of the symptoms of their stress to the detriment of longer-term coping. Both of the examples given in the previous section typify this reaction. In addition, drug-taking, increased alcohol consumption and frenetic social activity are all used as strategies for 'taking themselves out' of their immediate situation, sometimes to the detriment of themselves and others.

4 *Lowered efficiency* Being in a crisis impairs the ability of the person or family to think through their situation, reduces their 'work rate' for relationships and problem-solving, and affects their concentration and levels of emotional energy – all of these features can affect the way a person is in the home or at work and can carry a crisis from one location (e.g. work) into another (e.g. home).

5 *Limited duration* By its very nature, a crisis situation is not going to last for a long time and is likely to be resolved in one of two ways: (a) there may be some dramatic attempt to confront the crisis – e.g. someone leaves home, suicide is attempted, or physical violence (either self- or other-directed) is attempted; (b) the crisis is dealt with through some form of retreat – the person most affected retreats into depression, has a nervous breakdown, resorts to alcohol.

These responses to crisis have a number of consequences for the way in which individuals and families react to their situation, as Murgatroyd (1985) observes. These include: (a) the fact that the individual or family stops looking for evidence about their situation which would help them more fully understand what is happening to them; (b) they cease to look for alternative ways of coping, preferring to maintain their fatalistic attitude; (c) they are unable to act effectively and purposefully upon advice and directives, often misinterpreting suggestions; and (d) they so rationalize their situation in irrational ways (see Chapter 5) that they make their situation difficult for others to understand. These four features, coupled with all the others documented by Puryear (1975), mean that individuals and families in crisis often do not seek help or they seek help from so many sources that they find the conflicting advice and guidance which they receive makes any action on their part impossible.

The implication of these observations is that families in crisis often cut themselves off from available support networks. This occurs as a result of their friends and colleagues noting that they are less sensitive to and willing to use advice offered – to the point at which the advice itself dries up. Friends not involved in the crisis often find it difficult to understand why the family is unable to review its situation more critically and objectively – as they can – and they end their efforts aimed at trying to encourage the family to do this. At a more emotional level, individuals within families who are experiencing a crisis often project their feelings on to others (see Chapter 4) and do so whilst engaged in high levels of self-pity. This means that friends and helpers are accused of having thoughts and feelings which they do not have and the helping process often feels 'combative'. Moreover, the inability of family members to detach themselves from their own experience leads to a curiously paradoxical situation in which the experience of intense emotion is denied by the person having this experience, despite the fact that the intensity of the experience is obvious to others. This paradoxical situation is often very difficult for family friends and helpers to cope with.

If we imagine these characteristics of the crisis experience to be present in different ways and strengths in one or more family members, then it soon becomes apparent that the family as a set (or system) of interlocking individuals has the potential for becoming unstable. Members may blame each other for the predicament in which the family finds itself; the feelings experienced by one member may be transferred to others; roles may be challenged and changed in unexpected ways; there may be a leadership struggle within the family; new cross-generational coalitions may emerge as a way of coping with the crisis, thus establishing new boundaries within the family which are of themselves difficult for other family members to cope with. It is not surprising, given these possible family reactions, that outsiders (friends or helpers) find the experience of working with such a family confusing, distressing and difficult.

There is another way of conceptualizing the experience of crisis which we have also found useful. Rather than considering the possible consequences of crisis for the person or family in terms of specific intellectual, emotional and behavioural actions, it is sometimes helpful to look at a crisis in terms of its impact on a person's sense of identity. A number of events, such as becoming unemployed, retirement, becoming a parent and getting divorced are described by sociologists as 'status passages'. The word 'passages' here is being used in a similar way to the way psychologists use the term 'feature of the developmental process'. The idea behind this notion is that these events mark out a transition between one image of self and another.

This point about transition boundaries is well made by Hart (1976) when writing about divorce. Hart suggests that 'marital breakdown is not a once-and-for-all event: it is normally an attenuated process and the precise point at which a person recognises complete dissociation from his partner in life is often hard to define.... "Being divorced" is often better thought of as *becoming* something....' It is as if the process of becoming single occurs in marriage through a series of 'mini-crisis' events during which the partners become gradually more and more alienated and separated from each other. These mini-crisis events can be thought of in terms of preparatory socialization for the passage from one status (being married) to the next (being divorced and becoming single). In such passages (that from marriage to divorce is here used as an example; similar processes apply to other situations, e.g. unemployment, retirement) there is an absence of role support as the person moves from one status to the next. Three reasons are offered for this lack of social support for such transitions: (a) the person does not actively seek the help of others; (b) friends and helpers withdraw support because they disapprove of the status transition; (c) friends and helpers, though neither approving nor disapproving of the status transition, feel that they cannot help because they lack the necessary expertise to deal with the situation. Another reason for families to be cut off from their social support network is because they are seeking to hide or mask their crisis in some way, hoping that by so doing their situation will change in some way. Whatever the reason for a lack of connectedness to social support, it is a common feature of families and individuals in crisis.

The Task of the Helper

Many who look at the helping process regard as essential the availability of time in which issues of importance can be explored, conflicts worked through and emotions expressed. Indeed, many of the processes we have outlined elsewhere in this book assume the availability of time and the commitment of an individual, subgroup or family to the helping process throughout that time. In crisis work, time is not available. Indeed, if any single word characterizes the helping process in crisis it is 'immediacy'. Thus the model of the helping process we offer here reflects the fact that the immediacy of the crisis creates its own imperatives for the helper.

One implication of this time-urgency in crisis work is that it changes the goals of the helping process. Whereas the goals of the other processes we have outlined here involve significant self-change of one kind or another, the goal in crisis work is first and foremost to restore active coping. Whilst this may provide subsequent opportunities for the teaching of new coping skills or for work on self-change, the restoration of active coping is the major goal of helping a family in crisis (Murgatroyd, 1982).

This specific goal for helping – the restoration of active coping – requires us to say a little more about coping processes than has been possible so far. In particular, we have found it helpful to familiarize ourselves with the important work of Richard Lazarus and his co-workers at the University of California at Berkeley. Lazarus and Launier (1982) define coping as 'efforts . . . to manage (i.e. master, tolerate, reduce, minimize) environmental and internal demands and conflicts . . . which tax or exceed a person's resources'. This suggests that coping can be one or other of two kinds: (a) an attempt to change a crisis situation for the better by either changing the environment or the way in which the situation is perceived, or (b) an attempt to manage the situation by better coping with the effects of stress without necessarily trying to change the situation in any fundamental way.

Such a conception of coping as that advanced by Lazarus and Launier suggests four elements of coping which have implications for helpers. These are as follows:

(a) *Coping refers to a process and not an outcome* This means that helpers have the task of understanding the way in which family members sought to cope with their crisis prior to their arrival so that they may better understand the extent to which their coping has contributed to their current situation.

(b) *Coping involves people in making conscious choices* Helpers therefore need to attend to the way in which family members made choices in the situation they found or created for themselves.

(c) *Coping involves people assessing feedback as to the success or failure of their coping* Helpers need to attend to the way in which family members deal with information about themselves and their relationships.

(d) *Coping is about the 'fit' between the person and his or her environment* The helper needs to examine the extent to which family members are aware of and are using the resources in their environment (e.g. social support) so as to examine the quality of the 'fit' between themselves and their environment.

These points are explored in more detail in later sections of this chapter.

Strategies and Tactics

Some mention has already been made of social resources – friends, community, professional helpers, etc. The model of coping outlined here also suggests that family members are making use of their own personal resources – thinking, feeling and behaviours. This provides a useful distinction between the strategies which they employ and the specific tactics which characterize these strategies. Tactics depend upon the resources available to the individual and family: they include personal resources, such as health, energy, problem-solving skills, beliefs, values, creativity, and also environmental resources, such as money, friends, access to community agencies, transport. Whilst a particular family member may not use all of the resources available, their very availability helps to shape and directs the way in which tactics are employed. Most critical in shaping the use of resources is the underlying stategy which the family member is seeking to use and the reaction of other family members to this strategy. Whilst a strategy may be explicit – e.g. to use resources so as to reduce the stress effects of some crisis – some features of this strategy may not be so explicit – e.g. to seek to reduce stress so as to aid denial or repression.

In our experience, drawing a distinction between tactics and strategy in this way is helpful in attempting to understand the difference between what a person is doing in terms of coping and why they are doing it. It is also often helpful for the person or family in crisis to explore these two questions.

Development and Change

Once the helper accepts that coping is a process and as such plays an active part in shaping the nature of crisis experiences for families and their members, a number of further insights emerge for the helper. In particular, the helper has to recognize the importance of the motives which family members bring to their experience of crisis. When a person in crisis seeks help he or she is often motivated to take some risk in his or her situation so as to maximize the potential of a crisis for change and development; others who seek help are motivated by a different concern – to be confirmed in their disability and helplessness and to be supported as a helpless person or family. The helper, through understanding the motives which family members bring to their coping behaviour, can recognize the potential each crisis situation has for transition and encourage them to be reframed in this way. Where the person, subgroup or family is motivated by a desire to stay in crisis and to be confirmed as helpless then this task is made considerably more difficult – the family members are resisting transition and defending against it with helplessness (see Chapter 4).

In this context, it is worth noting that a great deal of helping in educational and medical settings is concerned with exploring the implications of future decisions. In particular, the exploration of consequences and the effects that 'ripple' within a family as the decision one person might make is seen to affect other family members. There is a branch of counselling known as developmental counselling (Carkhuff and Berenson, 1970) which is clearly concerned with the promotion of anticipation as a way of coping with potential sources of stress and distress.

Anticipation and Coping

A large number of individuals and families do not experience crises. They have developed a repertoire of coping actions which either enable them to diffuse the potential which a situation has for being a crisis very rapidly or to anticipate such situations long before they arise and avoid them. Such a repertoire of coping actions can be regarded as a set of anticipatory coping skills.

In the terms used earlier in this chapter, 'anticipation' is a form of coping strategy. Using it, families and the individuals within them seek to use problem-solving skills (see Chapter 5) in such a way as to evaluate future events, explore the risks inherent in current events, maximize the use of available coping resources (including social support networks) and build relationships within the family which constitute a family-helping network in itself. By so doing they are able directly to affect the situation in which they find themselves, enhance their own self-understanding and promote what might be called 'hardiness'.

Since some families and individuals adopt such a strategy, why is it that not all families and individuals do so? Putting this another way, why is it that some families are 'hardy' and some are not? This is an issue explored by a number of researchers, especially Suzanne Kobasa and her co-workers in Chicago and Leonard Pearlin and Carmi Schooler (Pearlin and Schooler, 1978; Kobasa and Puccetti, 1983). In addition to there being significant differences in the personality and orientation of 'hardy people' (those who rarely, if ever, experience events as crisis laden), there are some coping tactics which differentiate hardy and non-hardy individuals and families. Pearlin and Schooler (1978) have been especially helpful in identifying three features of the coping tactics which are used by non-hardy individuals which lead them to experience distress. The first concerns recognition – the non-hardy individual or family does not fully recognize the risks and crisis-laden features of the situations in which they find themselves. For example, a husband and wife might have a feeling that something is wrong in their relationship, but cannot identify just what it is. This lack of recognition impairs help-seeking and problem-solving and tends to perpetuate crisis-laden situations to the point at which a crisis is inevitable. The second feature of non-hardy individuals concerns skills. If the couple in the example just given did recognize that their difficulty revolved around different sexual attitudes or the wife's desire to have sex in a particular way which was being resisted by the husband, it may be the case that the partners do not possess the knowledge, skills or emotional strengths to modify or transform their situation. In such cases, the certain understanding of the situation and the recognition that a person or a family lacks the skills or strengths to deal with it intensifies the experience of helplessness and promotes the crisis. There is a third tactical feature of the non-hardy individual to which Pearlin and Schooler draw our attention. It is their tendency to deal with a stressful situation in one part of their lives by displacement. That is, a high stress experience in the family is dealt with by poor performance at work, thus creating and duplicating the stress. These tactical features do seem to suggest why some individuals and (in our experience) families are unable to use anticipatory coping.

There is a further reason why this strategy may not be used. A number of experiences which individuals and families find distressing – rape, motor accidents, death, illness, unemployment – are difficult and in some cases impossible to anticipate. Families and individuals which have hitherto been 'hardy' may find themselves in crisis when having to face up to the rape of their 17 year old daughter or the disfigurement of the father as a result of a motor accident.

These constraints on the use of the anticipatory coping strategy have a number of implications for helpers. The first is that the helper needs to develop an understanding of why anticipatory coping was not used as a strategy by the individual or family members with whom he or she is working. The helper might choose to encourage the development of such a strategy as a feature of the helping process he or she undertakes so that the family or individual is able to improve recognition or develop appropriate skills. This links to the second implication helpers might take from this discussion of hardiness – in developing a skill (e.g. problem-solving, contingency contracting, confrontation) as a response to a specific crisis situation there is a need for the helper to encourage members of the family to see these skills as being relevant to other circumstances. Helpers need to reinforce the value of anticipatory coping by linking current skills development to future events. This implies that the helper working on crisis issues needs to teach (Brandon, 1970; Murgatroyd, 1982). Finally, in these tasks the helper needs to be realistic about the abilities of family members to use the anticipatory coping strategies.

Coping with the Effects of Crisis – 'Buffer Coping'

If, for whatever reason, the anticipatory coping strategy is not being used by a family member or the family when faced with some crisis event, then a second strategy may be used. This we refer to as the 'buffer' strategy, following Pearlin and Schooler's observation that the essential feature of such a strategy is that the person or family in need seek to buffer themselves from the most distressing effects of their situation by changing its meaning. What was a crisis is now a difficulty; what was hitherto distressing becomes stressful.

What is most commonly involved in the pursuit of this strategy is the use of some cognitive restructuring or cognitive reinterpretation of the situation in which an individual or family finds themself. The way in which a situation is consciously thought about is changed so that its effects are seen to be less stressful. Within this strategy, a number of tactics are possible. We described in the previous chapter a form of rational–emotive restructuring of ideas and beliefs so as to change the meaning of the situation – some individuals or families in need discover a tactic of this kind for themselves. More commonly, however, individuals and family groups use one of two tactics. The first is referred to as *positive comparison*. In this tactic the person or family in distress compare their situation as favourably as possible with that of others so as to produce some feeling of 'it could be a lot worse'. For example, one of us has the experience of a close relative having to have a leg amputated. The day after the operation this person simply observed that the rest of the people in the ward in which he was a patient had had at least two limbs removed – he was 'the lucky one'. A second example concerns an unemployed father of six children who observed, 'Well, when my father was unemployed in the 1930s he did not get any income at all . . . now I have an earnings-related payment, child allowances and supplementary benefit . . . I don't like it, but it's much better than it was 50 years ago'. By comparing themselves with others in seemingly similar circumstances and producing a positive comparison the person or family is able to reinterpret their situation. A similar tactic is employed by others. We refer to this second tactic as *selective ignoring*. In this tactic the family or person in crisis chose to ignore the most distressing features of a situation and to cling on to that feature which they regard as offering them some (if modest) comfort. For example, the parents of a child who died in a motor-cycle accident comforted themselves for some considerable time with the thought that 'at least she died instantaneously'; the parents of a terminally ill cancer patient, at the moment of death, cautioned their grief by thinking, 'Well, at least now all that suffering is over'; the parents of a mentally handicapped child, whenever they experience doubt and uncertainty about their own coping, look to the child and remind themselves that 'at least he seems happy'.

These may seem like denials (in the latter tactic) and defence (in the former). This may well be one way of interpreting these tactics. The point to note is that these are *short-term* features of a strategy which is intended to create a breathing space for a couple, a family or an individual family member so that they can prepare themselves adequately to cope with their situation. If they persist to the point at which the reframing becomes unreal or ritualized, then defence and denial may well be appropriate descriptions of these tactics.

The role of the helper in supporting the family or person who seeks to use this 'buffer' strategy is to help them achieve a reframing of their thoughts which assists in the restoration of active coping in the short term without encouraging pretence or denial in the long term. In particular, the helper should work with the irrational beliefs that often emerge in crisis situations as a way of teaching the skill of reframing (see Chapter 5, pages 110–115).

Coping Through Stress Management

The two coping strategies described to this point – anticipation and buffering – are not as common as this third strategy. In our experience of crisis work, documented in Murgatroyd and Woolfe (1982) and Murgatroyd (1985), individuals and families most frequently seek to cope with the distress of crisis by dealing with each experience as it happens and by trying to work through that experience as it is happening. Many have developed elaborate tactics to enable them to do this: physical fitness, the ability to use friends and relatives and the use of meditation. But most commonly we have found that the following tactics are used:

(a) *Time will heal* The person or family 'grins and bears' whatever the situation gives rise to since they feel and think that the situation 'can only get better'.
(b) *Fatalism* The family or the person in need simply lives with and accepts the events of some crisis as they unfold, since it is felt that either there is nothing to be done about them or that 'it was meant to be'.
(c) *Avoiding confrontation* Even though one or more members feel that the situation would resolve itself if some kind of confrontation was to take place, this does not happen since they 'don't want any more aggravation' or 'I can't cope with the idea that it might not work'.
(d) *Waiting for something to turn up* The family or the person in need, like Mr Micawber, expects something to happen at any moment which will transform the situation: a good example of this being the husband who is told by the senior registrar that his son died during childbirth but who hopes the consultant will have some better news.
(e) *The morality version* Regarding the distress, pain and hardship associated with being in a crisis as a moral virtue.
(f) *Retreat or withdrawal* The person or family retreats from the situation by leaving the area, becoming ill, or developing so many contacts with helpers that they can blame the helpers for their predicament.

The common feature of all these tactics is that they do not seek to deal with the situation itself or to use the situation as a basis for self-change or family development. Instead, these are all forms of reaction to events as they unfold. They aim, however indirectly, to change the immediate effects of the crisis without necessarily affecting that crisis or their consequent experience of it in any way.

For the family focused helper there is a particular version of this strategy which is worth noting here. A number of families who find themselves 'in crisis' adopt this strategy, but different family members use different tactics to achieve the satisfactions of this strategy. For example, Dick and Sheila and their children have recently discovered that they are suffering from a rare and untreatable tropical illness which, in seven out of 10 cases leads to death. Dick constantly believes that something will turn up; Sheila believes that 'this is how our lives were meant to be'; Fred (aged 17) says he 'just doesn't believe the diagnosis' and that 'it will all turn out to be something simple, like diphtheria or something'; and the two twin girls (aged 15) have taken to their beds to be ill, despite the fact that the symptoms are spasmodic rather than constant. The helper in this case, through recognizing the overall strategy of the family, is better able to understand the specific tactics adopted by the individuals within it.

The role of the helper when faced with this strategy is to use his or her facilitative skills of empathy, warmth and genuineness (see the Preface, page xv) to encourage those with whom he or she is working to: (a) more readily accept the seriousness of their situation; (b) recognize that their own responses to the situation in which they find themselves help to shape that situation and that the adoption of a different tactic could change the nature or meaning of the situation in a way which might be beneficial to them; and (c) teach and promote the effective use of relevant ideas, behaviours or skills. In short, the helper's task is to expose the purely short-term value of this strategy and encourage the adoption of more effective long term coping.

It is worth noting that there are some effective ways of using this strategy with persons in crisis. For example, if the situation in which they find themselves is so distressing that they feel that they can no longer think objectively about it and that they therefore act impulsively in a way which is subsequently distressing to them, the helper can encourage them to use some form of relaxation training (Hewitt, 1982) to provide them with an immediate way of distancing themselves from the situation which they find themselves in 'here and now'; then the helper needs to teach them the use of some assertiveness skills (to give time for them to think carefully) and some decision-making skills (to encourage careful thinking). The strategy is not without value, but needs to be seen as a stepping-stone rather than as an end in itself.

The Role of the Helper

So far in this chapter, emphasis has been given to the importance of the helper examining the way in which a family or its members understand their situation, the ways in which they seek to cope with it and the meaning they attribute to their own coping. The aim is that the helper should come to understand the experience of crisis in the context of the coping strategy adopted by the family and its members.

The helper's achievement of this task will require him or her, as in other forms of helping, to display empathy, warmth and genuineness; to encourage positive transference; to seek to be concrete and direct in the way he or she handles the issues presented. In addition, the helper will need to negotiate a specific form of contract about the helping relationship with those whom he or she is seeking to help – a point returned to below (and also in Chapter 7). This is not very different from what occurs in other, more protracted and less immediate forms of helping. But, despite these similarities, there are important points of difference between helping in crisis and helping a person with needs which are not crisis-laden. For example, crisis work is characterized by both time-urgency and high intensity; other forms of helping can often take place over many months and can vary in levels of intensity. A second example concerns the work of the helper as skill teacher or educator – something that some other forms of helping (but not all) do not envisage. The aim of helping in crisis work is to restore active coping and, if time permits, enhance the coping repertoire of the family by so doing; other forms of helping are concerned with long-term personality change or with more than the restoration of coping. Whilst crisis work can lead to other, less time-urgent forms of helping, it is important that the helper him- or herself recognizes that the nature of helping *is* different in these respects from other forms of helping.

The recognition of these differences has led to some crisis-oriented helpers to seek to clarify the specific tasks which helpers need to perform when working with individuals or families who have crisis experiences. In our own work (reviewed more extensively in Murgatroyd and Woolfe, 1982, and in Murgatroyd, 1985) we have found the tasks suggested by Schwartz (1971) to be valuable and we present a summary of these tasks here. Whilst the summary is given in a logical order, it is rarely the case that these tasks can be separated in this way: they run together in the ebb and flow of difficult helping relationships. None the less, they provide a valuable framework for considering the role of the helper in families in crisis.

Task 1: *Help the family member(s) to face their crisis* The helper's first and most important task is to discourage denial and offer the family a clear statement of, analysis of and interpretation of the situation. The helper is aiming to encourage the family and its members to recognize the extent and nature of the crisis, their part in shaping this situation and their role in sustaining it. The helper is seeking to inject a high level of reality into their thinking.

Task 2: *Break up the crisis experience into manageable doses* The helper is seeking to reduce the overall impact of a complex situation so that he or she can encourage the members of the family to begin to feel that they can change their coping process in some way. One way of doing so is to see a crisis in terms of a series of interrelated, but none the less separate elements. By focusing upon each element, identifying possible actions relevant to that element and then sequencing responses to the various elements the helper can initiate some coping steps. Usually, the helper will find him- or herself having to work hard to break down a complex event into separate elements; it is also difficult for the helper to decide upon the sequence in which these elements will be tackled by the persons in need. None the less, this step is usually most valuable in reducing emotional intensity, promoting a degree of objectivity and enabling the family members involved to feel that some progress can be made.

Task 3: *Stop guessing and wishful thinking and promote objectivity* A major task of the helper when working with a family or some of its members who are experiencing crisis is to promote objectivity and a reality focus. To do so, helpers need to promote problem-solving skills. These include: fact-finding, brainstorming and option-listing, consequence evaluation and decision making. In promoting these in relation to the specific crisis that is current for the family, the helper needs also to reinforce the idea that these skills have a more general value. In this work the helper is acting as educator as well as facilitator.

Task 4: *Avoid false reassurance* Helpers, like those they are seeking to help, need to maintain a reality focus in their work if they are not to become a part of the crisis themselves. One practice that helpers need to guard against is offering false reassurances, especially about the consequences of some intended action or about the progress a family is making in its attempt to promote active coping. This is not to say that the helper should suspend warmth and acceptance – reassurance as to the helper's acceptance of family members as people needs constantly to be given; what is being said here is that this need for warmth and acceptance should not override the reality focus and genuineness of the helper.

Task 5: *Discourage projection* It is common for people in crisis to project blame on to others and to blame themselves for actions actually taken by others. So as to encourage those in need to focus on the present and the future and to minimize the extent to which the past dominates the helping process, the helper needs to encourage those with whom they are working to own their own problems and to act as if the problem was created the moment they sought help. Apportioning blame is unhelpful and counter-productive to helping in a crisis situation. If the helper fails to do this, he or she will be blamed for those attempts at coping which are unsuccessful.

Task 6: *Help individuals to help themselves* The helper will typically only have a short association with a family or person in crisis (hours and days rather than weeks or months); the helper therefore needs to encourage those with whom he or she is working to better connect themselves to available social support networks – the family itself, friends, professional and voluntary organizations who possess appropriate helping skills and resources, etc. To enhance connectedness, helpers will often need to teach skills of effective help-seeking – asking for what is wanted, being explicit, being assertive, expressing doubts. In addition, this task suggests that helpers should ensure that the family itself is seen to be a resource for coping and should encourage family members participating in the helping process to identify directly the skills and resources available within the family.

Task 7: *Promote active coping* The aim of all of the previous tasks is to help the family and the helper arrive at a point in which it is possible for those seeking help to imagine themselves responding differently to the situation they find themselves in and to rehearse these different responses so that they become the actual responses the person engages in. The helper uses all of the previous tasks to create an environment in which it is safe to explore alternative forms of coping with a crisis and in which some of these alternative forms become the agenda for action which the family adopts. Whilst a variety of the helping processes outlined elsewhere in this book are of value to helpers in this task, the helper should bear in mind the principle that this task ends when the family members with whom he or she has been working find themselves better able to cope with their situation and no longer need the helper. Though many more helping tasks might remain, the restoration of some equilibrium to the family so that it can use its own coping responses is the major task of a helper when working with a family in crisis.

The listing provided by Schwartz (1971) and elaborated here is a logical summary of the tasks the helper faces. Our own experience suggests that it is an appropriate and useful statement, especially for those helpers who only occasionally find themselves in crisis situations.

One of the features of these tasks is the emphasis given to the role of helper as educator. Several specific educational tasks are envisaged (especially in task 3 and task 6). The helper as teacher is an important feature of crisis work. This means, of course, that this helping process is more directive than some of the other processes outlined in this text. It requires the helper occasionally to take charge of the situation and to structure the experience of the family members with whom he or she is working so as to permit some progress to be made. There are clear dangers in this work: helpers need to avoid assuming that they can act through a family as if they were responding to the situation which was happening to them. It is not. Helpers also need to recognize that the crisis for a family often arises because they have not sought help before and should recognize that they, in providing some structure and direction, are shaping the family's expectations of other helpers.

One feature of crisis work that helpers need to attend to is the contract that they have with those they are helping. Murgatroyd (1985) suggests that agreement over a working contract is a vital first stage in a helping relationship with a person, couple or family in crisis – it provides a focus on reality and is concerned with establishing clear boundaries. Such a contract needs particularly to cover questions of accessability – just how and when can those in need contact the helper; time – just how much time is the helper able to afford the family and its individual members; responsibility – just what responsibility is the helper taking for the actions of the family. A failure to work within such a contract makes the helper vulnerable to frequent contact, to harassment by certain members of a family over the action of others and to accusations that he or she is responsible for any failures that arise in the family's attempts to cope. Contracts do not need to be elaborate, but they do need to be explicit.

A great deal of work in helping a person or family in crisis is concerned to increase the coping repertoire of the family. Work by Kobasa and Puccetti (1983), Pearlin and Schooler (1978) and Folkman and Lazarus (1982) all suggests that the hardiness of a person is a function of the variety of coping strategies and tactics he or she is able to call upon. This strongly supports the Minuchin (1974) contention that families who are flexible are less likely to experience distress than those who are rigid or chaotic when faced with challenge or change.

One way of thinking about crisis helping is that it is a starting point for moving the family or some of its members from being chaotic or rigid to being more flexible in their approach to change; in so doing, the helper also seeks to strengthen family cohesion by marking out boundaries between family members, the coping skills they possess and the coping strategies they employ. In addition, the helper needs to understand the psychodynamic qualities of the family in crisis, especially the tendencies within the family towards transference and projection, if he or she is to offer a clear statement of the family's situation and an analysis of its members' coping strategies. Finally, the helper needs to promote certain behavioural coping skills – especially problem-solving and help-seeking – so as to encourage the restoration of active coping. This way of thinking about crisis helping suggests that the helper needs to be especially able to utilize the ideas and processes outlined elsewhere in this text. In addition, since crisis work frequently involves the helper in enhancing the connection of a family to available social support networks, some of the issues about community work raised in Chapter 1 are also relevant to this task.

Conclusion

In this chapter we have outlined the nature of the helping process in the face of a family or individuals experiencing crisis. We have attempted to document some of the key tasks of this work, giving emphasis to the educative as well as facilitative roles which the helper might need to play. The aim of this work is to restore active coping. This is no easy task. Before embarking upon it, the helper needs to consider his or her own position both by having a clear and explicit contract with those with whom he or she is working and by having some form of personal support from others. Families in crisis engage in emotional discharge, and rightly so: the helper too needs to discharge his or her feelings about working with the family to someone who can help him or her cope with the task of crisis helping.

7

PROBLEMS IN HELPING FAMILIES

Introduction

So far in this book we have outlined the nature and sources of distress and examined some of the forms of helping that can be used to help families and their members reduce their experience of distress and promote more effective ways of coping. In particular, attention has been given to ways of affecting the family's communication system, the psychodynamics of family life and the behaviour which individuals engage in. In addition, we have looked at the special role of the helper in working with a family experiencing a crisis. In this final chapter we aim to document some of the practical difficulties which face helpers who are working with family members or whole families. The chapter is arranged under three headings, reflecting three basic stages in the helping process. These are: (a) the problems associated with 'setting-up' or establishing a relationship between the helper and those with whom he or she is working – the problem of beginnings; (b) the problems associated with sustaining the ongoing process and continuing helping – the problem of the process itself; and (c) the difficulties and problems associated with ending a helping relationship and understanding the consequences that particular relationship has had for both the family and the helper – the problem of completion.

Some of the difficulties we explore here are not unique to those helpers who adopt a family focused orientation for their work. After all, as we pointed out at the beginning of this text (see pages xii–xiv), the difference between family focused and individually focused helping is not so much one of technique as orientation: it is not surprising, therefore, that many of the practical difficulties are similar when the techniques are applied to families. Since some of the techniques and processes we have described are also used in community focused work, it is not surprising that many of the difficulties we shall outline will readily translate into this setting too. What is useful to note, however, is that the problems associated with family work are often multiple: the family itself creates distress and difficulty for the helper.

In the Preface to this book we emphasized the importance of the helper seeking to build a climate of trust and warmth within which they could work to promote family focused helping (see page xv). From time to time throughout this text this has been emphasized as a critical feature of helping and a prerequisite for the success of the practical processes we outline. For example, in describing the use of paradoxical intention (see pages 61–62) we gave emphasis to Hayley's observation that the first prerequisite for its successful use was the existence of an atmosphere of trust and understanding between the helper and those with whom he or she is working. A failure to achieve this trust is likely to render attempts to use this and other techniques ineffective and thus create further distress for both the helper and the family members.

In building such a trusting relationship, the helper needs effectively to communicate the four core conditions of helping. These are: (a) *empathy* – the ability to understand the distress of another person as if it were one's own without ever losing the 'as if' quality; (b) *warmth* – the ability to 'prize' and show acceptance of others without imposing conditions or overwhelming them; (c) *genuineness* – the ability to be honest, direct and 'straight' with the family members with whom one is working in a way that is sensitive to their needs but not manipulative; and (c) *concreteness* – the ability to retain the attention of the family members on the issues, processes and concerns central to the helping task at that time. These core conditions, as they are known (Nelson-Jones, 1982), suggest other facets of the helping process which the helper needs to attend to. For example, they suggest that the helper should ask open rather than closed questions, should actively listen and attend to all that is being said, should use silence as a way of accepting the family members and their needs, and should be concerned to give feedback and to structure the experience so as to promote concreteness. We do not intend to explore these in detail here (but see Munro *et al.*, 1983); rather, we wish to acknowledge the fact that if the core conditions are not being communicated the difficulties we outlined here will be unduly exacerbated.

Problems with Beginnings

When a helper begins to be involved with a family, one of its subgroups or an individual family member, a variety of questions arise which need to be resolved early if the process of helping is not later to become a part of the family's problems rather than an aid to the reduction of distress.

The first of these questions is '*Why is the helper helping?*' There are many reasons why a particular helper becomes involved with a particular family at a particular time. Social workers or education welfare officers, for example, often have a legal duty to become involved with a family in order to protect some person within that family or to act to prevent some deterioration in the overall well-being of the family. Other helpers, such as doctors, social workers, psychologists or counsellors, become involved with a family or some of its members because the family requests such an involvement. Other helpers become involved at the invitation of some third party – neighbours, friends. Finally, some helpers are involved with the process of helping because they are themselves friends of the family and are concerned to assist a family resolve some conflict, overcome or reduce distress, or meet some challenge or crisis. In helping, it is important to begin with some clear statement of the basis for being involved with a family and of the limitations that such an involvement brings. The social worker who is acting as an agent of a court, for example, will have a different form of relationship to the family than a social worker who is called in by the family to help with a specific difficulty. The helper should ensure that all family members likely to be affected by his or her involvement are clear as to the nature of that involvement. Indeed, it is a consequence of seeking to be genuine in a helping relationship that the helper should seek to be explicit about the reasons for his or her work.

A related question here is '*How has the family come to be helped?*' As has already been mentioned, some families actively and voluntarily seek out helpers so that their distress can be reduced; others are sought out by the helpers whose professional role requires them to act in some interventionist way, whether or not the family members wish them to do so. For example, the courts may instruct a social worker or probation officer to take some kind of action; the health authorities require the homes of families recently becoming parents to be visited by a midwife and a doctor; health visitors are expected, in most areas, to undertake routine checks on the health of children; officers of the National Society for the Prevention of Cruelty to Children (NSPCC) may have reason to visit a family in response to the suggestion by neighbours that the parents are being cruel to or are physically punishing their children. These are all different kinds of voluntary and involuntary involvements with helpers. What is more, help seeking can be much more complex. For example, Mr and Mrs Gale and their son Richard went to a general practitioner to discuss their son's stammer; the general practitioner referred them to a clinical psychologist who in turn referred them to an educational psychologist working in a speech therapy research unit recently established at a nearby college. The family are not unhappy with these moves between helpers, but it is important that the helpers are aware of the moves the family has made in getting to them. This is important for two reasons. First, many families who obtain help from one source (e.g. a social worker) may also be receiving help from other sources (e.g. a doctor, psychologist or voluntary counsellor). In order to minimize confusion and reduce the level of conflict between the actions of one helper and those of another, it is essential to know which helpers are being seen by which members of a given family. The second reason for this issue to be regarded as important concerns motivation: if the family is voluntarily seeking help then the motivation of its members to act in a way the helper is seeking to encourage is higher than if they are involuntarily involved in the helping process. Since motivation is crucial to the helping process – a point made on several occasions in this text – it is essential that both helper and helped are clear about the basis for their work.

The critical difference between those family members who have volunteered to seek help and those who feel obliged to attend for help concerns their willingness to self-disclose, their willingness to respond to confrontation and challenge and their willingness to persist with the helping process when this itself becomes distressing, as it can be (see Chapter 3, page 60). Different motivations for help-seeking will lead to different responses from family members to these concerns. Notice that we do not suggest that family members have to be legally required to seek help before these issues become important to the process of helping. The variable is whether or not the family member *feels* obliged rather than *is* obliged to seek help. Not all members of a given family will think and feel the same way about help-seeking. For example, if only one member of a family is seeking help others may regard this as a betrayal; if all but one member is seeking help, then the one member may feel a 'victim' in some sense. These observations suggest that it is important for the helper to be clear about how each family member feels about being helped – a failure to be clear about this may lead the helper to be over-optimistic about what can be achieved or to be diverted into tasks which could have been dealt with more appropriately in some other way.

The fact that different family members experience different motives for help-seeking raises a third question here, namely *'Who should constitute the family to be helped?'* In some of the materials presented here it is clear that those who have most influence on the family's dynamics are those who only occasionally visit the family – grandparents or aunts, for example, are mentioned specifically in an earlier section dealing with coalitions and boundaries (see Chapter 3, pages 53–55). Should the helper attempt to incorporate these persons into the helping process? Should the helping activities take place at times which would maximize the potential of these persons attending? What are the effects upon the helping process of a significant family member – the father, for example – not being present? How many family members does a helper feel comfortable with when working – do the children need to be involved? The response to such questions depends upon the nature of the issues facing the family, the structure of the family and the skills of the helper. Though it is possible, as Murray Bowen and others have suggested (see Chapter 1, page 7), to work with a family through just one member of that family, it is difficult to do so when that family is seen to be detached or chaotic (see Chapter 3). We stress throughout this book that the family focused form of helping is an orientation – it is about the way in which the helper conceives distress as residing in the family's interactions and dynamics; it is not about the actual number of people present when a helping activity is taking place. None the less, the helper does need to make clear his or her assumptions about those who will be involved in the process and the consequences of them failing to attend.

Related to this last question is the question that arises early in both the thinking of the helper and that of those whom he or she is seeking to help. It is *'How long will this all last?'* The duration of the helping process will vary from family to family, depending again upon the difficulty presented, the motivation of the family members to work and the skills of the helper. Just as it is important to clarify the motives of participants and the framework of helping, so it is important to establish some time-frame in which the helper *intends* to work – it can be amended by negotiation in the light of experience.

But experience strongly suggests that having a clear time-frame within which they know the process is to take place acts as a strong motivating force to those seeking help.

The final question we offer here concerns the role taken by the helper. Putting this as a single question is difficult, since a number of separate points need to be made. From the point of view of the family members, the question often arises in the form: 'You are going to tell us what to do about it all, aren't you?' – implying some sort of directive–advice-giving model of the helping process. From the helper's viewpoint, the question usually takes the form 'What is the most appropriate role for me to perform on this occasion?' Our experience is that many of those who seek help have unrealistic expectations of the skills of the helper, an unrealistic expectation about what can be completed in a short time and an expectation that they will be given firm and clear directives about how they should respond to their situation or a statement about who is to blame. Yet often the helper is merely seeking to encourage the family members to explore their own distress, to develop insights into the way in which they have contributed to the creation of this distress and to understand more directly the way in which their relationships with other people are maintaining this distress. The helper is seeking to encourage self-help rather than giving direction; is encouraging new learning and the development of enhanced coping rather than trying to 'deal with' a situation. There can therefore be a tension between the expectations that family members have about the role of the helper and the actual process of helping the helper chooses to use. This tension can sometimes be productive, but it can also lead to an untimely and unintended end to the helping process or to confusion, uncertainty and a fragmenting of relationships within the family. Helpers, therefore, need to make clear the basis on which they intend to work with a family and to feel sure that the family has an understanding of the meaning and implications of this role.

These comments about the beginning phase of the helping process lead to a major and essential feature of the helping process: the establishment of contracts. By 'contract' here we do not mean a legally binding document signed by all participants and witnessed by observers; rather, we suggest that it is essential that the helping process begins with a clear statement of the tasks faced by all of the participants engaged in that process.

The kinds of contracts which a helper can negotiate with those with whom they are working will vary. Much will depend upon the nature of the problems presented by family members and the decisions the helper consciously makes about the helping task (see Chapter 1). Usually the contract will cover such matters as time (both the total period in which helping will take place and the duration of each helping session), the role of the helper, and the tasks of the family members who attend. In addition, some contracts will need to make clear that homework will be expected of those engaged in the helping process (especially relevant to contingency contracting, assertiveness, cognitive behaviour modification and some forms of communications intervention). It is also useful, when setting and negotiating a contract, to have some clear indication of how the contract will terminate. For example, it might be agreed that the contract will end in two months or sooner if family members all agree that significant progress has been made. Some contracts will need to make clear what access family members can have to the helper outside agreed contact times – can they telephone the helper at work or at home, can they 'drop in' to see the helper at different times? The need for an access 'clause' is especially important in crisis helping. For some families, the question of using other helpers will also need to be discussed. We have mentioned elsewhere (see Chapter 6, page 131) that some families exploit the helping network as a means of displacement or as a means of obfuscating the underlying issues which face them. The helper will need to decide, if it is an appropriate question, what links he or she will have with others who are working with the family members and will need to disclose these links to the family.

The negotiation and setting of such a contract is an important step for three reasons. First, the establishment of boundaries between the helper and the family is important in avoiding undue conflict and confusion later in the helping process. Many difficulties which arise in the ongoing process – such as those concerned with access or confusion about the importance of homework assignments – can be avoided if the helper is clear about these points at the beginning. Second, the elements of a contract are important in preserving the nature of the helping relationship – failure to be explicit about the helping role can lead to exploitation or an attempt by the family to incorporate the helper into their communication system. Finally, contracts are valuable to family members in establishing a framework within which it is safe to self-disclose, to experiment with new coping skills or to express negative emotions. The absence of an explicit contract fosters uncertainty and repression.

Simply stating that contracts are important does not remove the practical difficulties associated with the agreement over a contract or with maintaining a contract once agreed. Time needs to be taken after a period of observation and assessment by the helper to discuss the need for a clear contract, to specify the elements of that contract which are important to the helper and to negotiate and discuss the elements of the contract which the family members engaged in the helping process wish to be included. Having said this, a contract is not a weapon: it is a device which, in our experience, facilitates the helping process.

Some helpers ask, 'What if a contract is broken?' For example, let us imagine that a helper sees as critical to his or her strategy the keeping of a diary by family members of the arguments which they have during the course of a week. If this diary is not kept by all family members, what reaction should the helper have to the situation? Our reaction is that this tells the helper a lot about the family members and about their relationships with others. It suggests that there is a need for the helper to disclose directly to the family his or her reactions to this development and to see it as a basis for exploring the meaning of the helping contract with the family. In this sense, contracts tell the helper a good deal about motivation and commitment and have the potential for illuminating the family's own internal structure. Significant breaches of the contract require the helper and the family members with whom they are working to re-examine their relationship and re-establish or modify their contract.

Problems with the Ongoing Helping Process

In describing some of the practical problems in establishing a helping relationship it was noted that how such a relationship is established will affect both the ongoing helping process and its outcomes. In this section of the chapter we examine some of the difficulties which arise once the process is well and truly under way.

The first and most obvious difficulty is establishing just what the needs of the family members are and just which of these needs the helper is to regard as the focus for his or her work. A family may define their needs in a particular way – e.g. Jack (aged 6) is still bedwetting, Sally (aged 14) stutters, Bob (the husband) has to have sex in a particular way at particular times and his wife is refusing now to cooperate, 'We all are very depressed . . .' – but the helper may regard all these needs statements as superficial and feel a need to 'look behind the mask' at the family's rules, rituals and games, at their psychodynamics or at the chain of stimulus–response–reinforcement which gives rise to such statements in the first place. How does the helper shift the focus from Jack, Sally, fetishism or depression to the family's communications, psychodynamic features or behaviour? Indeed, how does the helper recognize what the underlying issues are, given that the family members are being quite firm in their insistence that 'All is well, except . . .' Jack's bedwetting, Sally's stutter, the husband's fetishism and the feeling of depression?

The questions posed here imply that the helper needs time to reflect upon and seek to understand the family's basic processes. Sometimes this is achieved through the observation of how those present interact with each other; sometimes it is obvious from the way one family member speaks of all other members; sometimes the helper is able to discern the patterns from what is not said rather from what is said. Whatever 'access' the helper has to the family *as a family*, he or she needs to look carefully at the patterns displayed and to listen to the subtle and hidden messages of the words used by those he or she is seeking to help. In addition, he or she needs to question critically those presenting for help about their definitions and interpretations of their 'problem' and to try and set such definitions and interpretations into a broader context.

To make this point clear, the helper needs to ask questions such as: What is it about the pattern of communication in the family which makes bedwetting a form of communication for Jack? What patterns of reinforcement is Sally obtaining which sustain her stuttering? What transference and projections are involved in the wife seeking help over her husband's fetishism? Is the family which is depressed more cohesive when depressed than when 'normal' – what reinforces 'being depressed' in this family? What these questions, and others like them, lead us to is the suggesion that the helper needs to develop some understanding, some hypothesis about the family's problem that goes beyond description. In a sense, the family focused helper needs to develop some hypothesis about the family which he or she can test against contacts with individuals, subgroups or the family as a whole and then revise in the light of experience. Family focused helpers are thus family focused researchers, seeking to explain the actions of the family by reference to a hypothesis. Some, especially Mara Pelazzoli and her co-workers in the Milan 'school' of family therapy (Pelazzoli *et al.*, 1978), suggest that it is important to offer a hypothesis to the family members with whom one is working as early as possible and to offer a positive connotation of this hypothesis (see Chapter 3, pages 43–44).

Forming a hypothesis is difficult, even if the helper is able to spend considerable time with the family *in toto*. Most commonly, helpers work with an individual or a subgroup of the family and have only limited 'data' upon which to base their hypothesis. None the less, the development of a structured understanding of the position of these individuals or the subgroup within the family will enable the helper to formulate some statement about the dynamics of the family which is sustaining distress. To do this effectively, the helper will need to have given thought to the various features of family dynamics – communications, rules, roles, rituals, boundaries, transference, projection, repression and behaviour – which we have explored in this text. The helper will also need to take full account of the family's own hypothesis about its situation.

There are two special difficulties worth mentioning here. The first concerns the nature of the models available to the helper which may influence the way in which they inform his or her understanding and hypothesis about the family. A great deal of the work reflected in this text and in the literature on families generally is derived from studies of white, English-speaking, upper working-class and middle-class families; indeed, a substantial body of theory derives from work with American families who are 'in therapy' – a term which has its own special cultural connotations in the United States. There are dangers in translating these ideas and models from one culture to another, as Murgatroyd (1984) has observed. We know little about the different cultural assumptions, patterns of interaction or behavioural shaping elements in the families of Muslim, West Indian, Rastafarian, Eastern European or Asian families or of homosexual couples and families. We therefore need to exercise care in translating these models from one cultural group to another.

The second difficulty concerns the helper's own perspectives. For a variety of reasons, helpers tend to become attached to a single school of thought about the nature of helping. Whilst this has certain advantages (not least of which is the development of specific competences), there is a major disadvantage. It is that an understanding of the position of an individual, family or subgroup of a family is made to 'fit' the dominant models of this school rather than these models being adjusted, modified or abandoned in favour of the family, individual or subgroup. In other words, helpers may seek to 'fit' the situation in which they find themselves to some pre-existing hypothesis, sometimes in an inappropriate way, and in so doing pose a threat to those they seek to help (Murgatroyd, 1981). As Walrond-Skinner suggests, helpers working in a family focused way need a repertoire of skills, ideas and resources which they can apply flexibly and imaginatively in each case. We share here her concern to promote a skilled and structured eclecticism for family focused work.

One of the reasons why it is important for helpers to advance hypotheses or statements of their own which reflect their understanding of the family's situation is that by so doing they sharpen the boundary between themselves and other family members. A hypothesis about the processes used by the family which is openly advanced 'marks the helper out' from family members who often do not reflect upon such processes. The establishment of such a boundary between helper and family members is important, since the helper will have only a temporary involvement in the emotional and transactional life of the family and his or her role needs to be delineated as much as possible. But there is another reason for seeking to establish boundaries. It is that by so doing the helper reduces the extent to which individuals, subgroups or the family as a whole seek to incorporate the helper into their own systems of communication. Individuals and subgroups often seek to recruit helpers in taking sides against other individuals or subgroups. Families as a whole sometimes seek to incorporate the helper into their family system so that, for all practical purposes, they neutralize the potential for helping that his or her involvement brings. Both of these scenarios pose difficult problems for helpers. What is at stake is the ability of the helper to reflect upon the family *and their own role within it* so as to retain both a reality focus and a sense of objectivity. The loss of this detachment leads to the helper colluding with the family or one of its subgroups or an individual family member and so perpetuates the family's distress. Offering a hypothesis, marking out boundaries and retaining objectivity through detachment are important features in the ongoing helping process.

Working with families can be a difficult task. One of the features of family work where two or more family members are involved is that the helper has him- or herself to cope with the simultaneous discharge of emotion by several people. Helping families through two or more family members has a high potential for (a) emotional discharge on a 'grand' scale; (b) conflict in which the helper is encouraged to feel both a persecutor ('You're making him get upset . . . we came here to stop crying and all you do is make us cry and feel unhappy') and a victim ('It's your fault that we're not making progress . . .'); (c) the helper feeling that progress is made difficult by the different levels of acceptance of his or her role by different family members. Working with individual family members in a family focused way carries similar difficulties and some others – in particular, the difficulty of knowing just how valuable is this person's own understanding of his or her own position within the family. The point is that working in a family focused way creates a need for helpers to make their own arrangements for support and supervision so that they themselves can retain their detachment, a sense of objectivity and a boundary.

The term 'supervision' is used here not to imply some hierarchical management of helping. Rather we use it in the sense in which it is used in psychotherapy, namely as a vehicle by which a helper is able to discuss, share, explore and examine with another person the nature of the problems with which he or she is dealing, the helper's own role, and the ideas which he or she may have for future actions. The role of this 'other' person is to offer critical comments, to support, to aid reflection, to share experiences and to make suggestions in a spirit of mutuality and concern for the helper. Supervision is a means for showing support for the helper so as to sustain him or her in the helping task (Hess, 1980).

The need for supervision in part concerns the need to retain some objectivity about the helping process. But it is also concerned with the 'self' of the helper. When a helper works with an individual family member or a part of the family or the family as a whole, he or she is aiming to encourage some critical self-reflection: implicit in this task is the fact that the helper will be required to self-reflect too. Sometimes this process of reflection triggers some unresolved issues for the helper; sometimes the helper will feel angry or frustrated, yet he or she may not feel able to share these feelings when they arise since to do so would be counter-productive to the task in hand; sometimes, issues are raised which the helper has previously and painfully had to work through him- or herself. In these kinds of circumstances, support through supervision is a way of exploring the implications of helping for the helper as a person. A failure to do so can lead to the helper's own needs being unduly confused with those of the family members with whom he or she is working.

These three reasons – self-awareness, support and discharge – are strong reasons for the helper making some specific arrangements for supervision. To those who remain doubtful, let us add another. Support and supervision provide a basis for the development of the skill of the helper. In part this results from two people looking at the ways in which the helping process might develop, thus sharing skills and perspectives; in part this comes from the process of self-disclosure by the helper. In self-disclosure there is often insight into the underlying family process with which the helper is most concerned. Organizations seeking to offer helping services, such as voluntary groups or professional helping agencies, need to bear these concerns in mind and to make adequate arrangements for support and supervision for their helpers (Murgatroyd, 1983).

Linked to the need for supervision is the helper's need to develop his or her personal resources to deal with frustration. In our experience, helper frustration takes two forms. These are (a) the frustration associated either with failure or with helping that 'gets stuck', and (b) the frustration that comes from acting effectively on the issue that the helper was first presented with but leaving untouched a host of other issues that emerged during the course of the helping process. This last frustration is essentially the helper's own thinking problem – it's 'just tough'. In writing a book, there is only partial satisfaction in completion – there is always more that could have been written, a better way of resolving some technical question, a clearer example or illustration, a better expression – but writing has to end at some point. It is just the same with helping. As for the first form of frustration, the helper has the task of sharing this feeling with those he or she is seeking to help and to discuss with them the nature of being 'stuck' or 'failing' and exploring the ways in which he or she might make more progress by changing the way in which they are working together or starting the same strategy anew. But helpers should caution themselves about holding the irrational belief that they 'must be thoroughly competent and achieving at all times' (see Chapter 5 and pages 111–115 – some failure is inevitable and, though frustrating, needs to be owned up to when it occurs and the helping process is ended.

The final point we make in this section concerns retaining the focus for the work of helping – what we have called 'concreteness' elsewhere in this chapter. When the helper feels frustrated, or when the family members are seeking to incorporate the helper into their communication system, or when the helping process involves high levels of emotional discharge, the helper has to keep in mind the task upon which he or she is engaged and what was agreed through the contract. Often, during the course of helping, other tasks suggest themselves. For example, what began as a problem of 17 year old Andrew's depression develops into the problem of Andrew's mother refusing to treat him as being old enough to make decisions for himself; this in turn becomes linked to the mother's own frustration over the career she never had because her parents refused to let her make decisions for herself. On how many of these issues does the helper work? Is there a danger of being diverted from the core concerns of the family and the hypothesis advanced by the helper into *culs-des-sacs* and alley-ways which prevent the major issues being worked through? The helper needs to maintain a concern with the central issue as defined in his or her hypothesis so that progress can be made and the helping process can continue to be ongoing.

Problems in Ending the Helping Process

At some point, the helping process will end. A critical question for the helper is *'How do I know that the end of the process has been reached?'* One answer to this question concerns contracts. If a contract has been negotiated which directly addresses the question of the duration of helping, then the helper is able to use this contract to review progress and to negotiate with those with whom he or she is working whether or not they wish to continue with the process. It may be at this point that the family members decide that their own objectives have been achieved and that there is no need for further work. Alternatively, they may decide that there is a need for further work and wish to continue the helping process. The helper then needs to encourage agreement about a second contract – is it to be simply an extension of the first (a renewal) or should it be extended or changed in some way? Contracts thus provide natural end points for the helping process, which is another reason why some helpers prefer to work with contracts rather than without them.

But even with a contract, the helper may feel that there is little more that he or she can offer and wish to end the process. Equally, those who are being helped may feel that, despite their initial agreement to a contract, they do not feel that further progress can be made and that the helping process should end. These scenarios suggest strongly that the helper should share his or her thoughts and feelings with the family members and examine the progress made during the helping process so as to ensure that all agree to termination. Persisting with a process simply because a contract exists is wholly inappropriate.

On many occasions it is family members who indicate their desire to terminate a helping relationship by their failure to attend agreed helping sessions. It is always best to give the family members a chance to explain their feelings and to encourage them to do so rather than automatically to assume that non-attendance indicates a desire to terminate the helping process (Nelson-Jones, 1983). If the family members do suggest ending the process and the helper feels that much is still to be done, then the helper needs to share his or her thoughts and feelings genuinely with the family and encourage its members to make a decision based on the 'best' possible information about his or her intentions for the future. This often involves the helper in recognizing that the family's definition of its needs differs from those envisaged by the helper – helpers will find themselves having to hold their tongues or contain their emotions when a family in which they have invested considerable intellectual and emotional energy decides for itself that it wishes to end the process.

A related question asked by helpers is '*How can I end a helping relationship without leaving those I am helping feeling rejected in some way?*' Our experience suggests that ending based on mutual agreement results from a careful and joint review of all that has happened in the helping relationship. In addition, the helper is able to reinforce points of learning, transition and change that have occurred since the relationship began. Indeed, an increasing focus upon transition learning – making connections between current learning and the future – suggests that those being helped are beginning to find ways of reconciling themselves to carrying the meaning and results of the helping relationship into the future. The helper can usefully work on transition learning as a feature of the ending of the helping process (Adams *et al.*, 1976).

The problem of rejection at the end of a helping relationship affects not only those being helped, but also the helper. This is especially the case when the helper feels that the process has been prematurely terminated. If the helper feels rejected, there are several questions that can usefully be explored through the relationship with his or her supervisor (see above). These include the following: What did I try to do and how well do I feel I did it? 'Did I take risks in this helping process and if I did, what did I learn by doing so? What did I learn from working with this individual or group of family members that will influence my subsequent work with others? These are important questions for helpers to ask themselves at the end of all helping relationships – they are especially important when the helper feels rejected. In our view, helping is a skill that needs continual updating and evaluation. A failure to explore such questions implies a smugness and complacency about helping and its meaning. Learning about helping is a form of learning about oneself, and as such is a life-long process.

When a helper feels that he or she is no longer best able to help an individual or group of family members, termination of the helping relationship is one option which must be faced. Another option is to refer the family or individual to other sources of help. Of course, referral to other helping organizations or individuals requires the helper to have an accurate appraisal of the needs of those he or she is seeking to help and to have an understanding of just why it is that he or she feels unable to help him- or herself. It also requires the helper to have a thoroughgoing knowledge of the available sources of help in the community, including an understanding of the resources, policies, programmes of work and limitations of particular helping agencies. Thus it is not good enough to know that a voluntary organization exists to help those recently bereaved; the helper needs to know something about the work of this organization, how individuals are received into it, what individuals can expect and not expect as a result of their association with the organization, and so on. Most frequently, referral is helped by knowing a person within an organization. Helpers should feel free to discuss the prospect of a referral with someone who is likely to receive the referral, taking care not to disclose the identity or any confidential material to that person. Such a discussion often helps the helper identify precisely why such a referral would be of value to the family members with whom he or she is working. Having established where and often to whom to refer the individual or family members, the helper then needs to explore with that individual or family the implications of a referral and his or her reasons for suggesting it. If a referral is agreed upon by the family members, then the helper should make clear and definite arrangements for the referral and should be especially clear about his or her own role once referral has taken place. For example, the helper needs to indicate whether he or she will continue to be available to the family or some of its members after the referral and to indicate the kind of information which he or she is going to pass to the person with whom they will now be working. Being clear about these points will reduce the extent to which a family or its members might feel rejected or 'shunted' by the referral process.

We have already suggested that helpers need to reflect in some way upon the work they have undertaken with a person, subgroup or family when that work comes to an end. Such an evaluation needs to include questions about style (Was I too direct? Did I overdo being friendly? Was I too technical in the language I used?), the use of specific skills (How could I have improved the use of, say, paradoxical intention, contingency contracting or the offering of some hypothesis about the family's psychodynamics?) and success (Whilst this family group has been helped in one area, what is left undone?). There are a variety of rating scales and checklists which helpers can use to develop systematic evaluations of their work (e.g. Cox, 1973, 1978) and valuable practical texts against which they can review their own activities (e.g. Nelson-Jones, 1983). Helpers can ask those they have helped to give feedback on their helping; other helpers can occasionally participate in helping work so as to give feedback and suggest skills to the helper; the helper can participate in in-service training and occasional workshops concerned with specific skills; helpers can read the various texts and journals concerned with helping processes, ideally having their own programme of directed reading; they can join professional and voluntary organizations for helpers which will provide updating and training opportunities; or helpers can make use of supervision arrangements to evaluate the impact of their work on others and to identify areas in which skill development might need to take place. Whatever combinations of these evaluation resources persons engaged in helping make use of, they should recognize that they have a duty to those whom they are helping to improve their skills and judgements. Indeed, we would suggest that evaluation is a vital process for helpers to engage in – a failure to do so is likely to render subsequent attempts at helping less effective than might otherwise be the case.

In passing, it is worth noting that family focused helping is a thoroughly researched form of helping. A review by Gurman and Kniskern (1978) and an analysis by Murgatroyd *et al.* (1985) strongly suggest that family focused helping is an especially effective process, most especially when it is focused upon the relationship between marital partners or the behaviour of children within the family (Duck *et al.*, 1984). Knowing that this orientation in helping is generally effective should not inhibit the helper questioning his or her own effectiveness in specific circumstances.

Conclusion

In this chapter we have explored some of the practical implications of the helping process for the helper. We have done so through thinking of this process as having definite phases: beginning, middle and end. Not all of the issues we have raised here will be equally important to those who engage in helping from a family focus – the issues we examine do, however, reflect our own experience of the process of helping and the experience of being a helper with its commensurate feelings of vulnerability, risk and satisfaction. Our conclusion, after several years of experience, is that working in a family focused way to help individuals and groups of family members reduce their distress is a rewarding (if at times exhausting) experience.

REFERENCES

Adams, J., Hayes, J., and Hopson, B. (1976) *Transition – Understanding and Managing Personal Change*. London: Martin Robertson.
Adlam, D., Henriques, J., Rose, N., Salfield, A., Venn, C., and Walerdine, V. (1976) 'Psychology, Ideology and the Human Subject.' *Ideology and Consciousness* **1**, 5–56.
Anderson, D. B. (1969) 'Nursing Therapy with Families.' *Perspectives in Psychiatric Care* **7**, 2–27.
Apter, M. J. and Smith, K. C. P. (1979) 'Psychological Reversals – Some New Perspectives on the Family and Family Communications.' *Family Therapy* **6**(2), 89–100.
Bandura, A. (1969) *Principles of Behaviour Modification*. New York: Holt.
Barker, P. (1980) *Basic Family Therapy*. London: Granada Publishing.
Bateson, G. (1956) 'Cultural Problems Posed by a Study of Schizophrenic Processes.' In *Schizophrenia – An Integrated Approach*, edited by A. Aureback. New York: Ronald Press.
Becvar, R. J. (1974) *Skills of Effective Communication – A Guide to Building Relationships*. New York: John Wiley.
Bettelheim, B. (1968) *Children of the Dream*. New York: Harper & Row.
Boszormenyi-Nagy, I. and Framo, J. (Eds) (1965) *Intensive Family Therapy*. New York: Harper & Row.

Boy, A. V. and Pine, G. P. (1980) 'Avoiding Counsellor Burn-out Through Role Renewal.' *Personnel and Guidance Journal* **59**, 161–163.

Brandon, S. (1970) 'Crisis Theory and Possibilities of Therapeutic Intervention.' *British Journal of Psychiatry* **117**, 627–653.

Bulkeley, R. and Sahami, V. (1984) 'Treatment of Longstanding Encopresis in a Twelve Year Old Boy Using Behaviour Modification Within a Framework of Systems Theory.' *Newsletter of the Association for Child Psychology and Psychiatry* **6**(1), 23–27.

Carkhuff, R. R. and Berenson, B. G. (1970) *Beyond Counselling and Therapy*. New York: Holt, Rinehart & Winston.

Carmody, T. P. (1978) 'Rational–Emotive, Self-instructional and Behaviour Assertion Training – Facilitating Maintenance.' *Cognitive Therapy Research* **2**, 241–254.

Central Statistics Office (1984) *Social Trends, 1984*. London: HMSO.

Clement, J. A. (1977) 'Family Therapy – The Transferability of Theory to Practice.' *Journal of Psychiatric Nursing* **15**(8), 33–37, 42–43.

Cochrane, A. L. (1972) *Effectiveness and Efficiency – Random Reflection on Health Services*. London: Nuffield Provincial Hospitals Trust.

Cooper, D. (1971) *Death of the Family*. Harmondsworth: Penguin.

Copermann, C. D. (1973) 'Aversive Counterconditioning and Social Retraining – A Learning Theory Approach to Drug Rehabilitation.' Unpublished PhD thesis, State University of New York.

Cox, M. (1973) 'The Group Therapy Interaction Chronogram.' *British Journal of Social Work* **3**, 243–256.

Cox, M. (1978) *Coding the Therapeutic Process – Emblems of Encounter, A Manual for Counsellors and Therapists*. Oxford: Pergamon.

Department of Health and Social Security (1984) *Children in Care in England and Wales*. London: HMSO.

Dobash, R. E., and Dobash, R. (1974) 'Violence Between Men and Women within the Family Setting.' Unpublished paper presented at the 8th World Congress of Sociology, Toronto, Canada.

Dryden, W. (Ed.) (1984) *Individual Therapy in Britain*. London: Harper & Row.

Duck, S., Lock, A., McCall, G., Fitzpatrick, M. A., and Coyne, J. C. (1984) 'Social and Personal Relationships.' *Journal of Social and Personal Relationships* **1**, 1–10.

Duhl, F. J., Kantor, D., and Duhl, B. S. (1973) 'Learning, Space and Action – A Primer of Sculpture.' In *Techniques of Family Therapy*, edited by D. A. Bloch. New York: Grune & Stratton.

REFERENCES

D'Zurilla, T. J. and Goldfried, M. R. (1971) 'Problem-solving and Behaviour Modification.' *Journal of Abnormal Psychology* 78, 197–226.
Eaton, M., Peterson, M., and David, J. (1976) *Psychiatry*. Flushing, N.Y.: Medical Examination Publishers.
Ellis, A. (1962) *Reason and Emotion in Psychotherapy*. New York: Lyle Stewart.
Erikson, E. H. (1959) *Identity and the Life Cycle*. New York: International Universities Press.
Erwin, E. (1973) *Behaviour Therapy – Scientific, Philosophic and Moral Foundations*. London: Cambridge University Press.
Eysenck, H. J. (Ed.) (1976) *Case Studies in Behaviour Therapy*. London: Routledge & Kegan Paul.
Folkman, S. and Lazarus, R. S. (1980) 'An Analysis of Coping in a Middle-aged Community Sample.' *Journal of Health and Social Behaviour* 21, 219–239.
Foucault, M. (1954) *Mental Illness and Psychology* (translated by Alan Sheridan). New York: Harper & Row.
Faulder, C. (1984) 'The Happy Ever After Syndrome.' *The Guardian*, 16 May 1984, p. 13.
Finer Report (1974) *The Report of the Committee on One-parent Families*, Cmnd 5629. London: HMSO.
Framo, J. (1965) 'Rationale and Techniques in Intensive Family Therapy.' In *Intensive Family Therapy*, edited by I. Boszormenyi-Nagy and J. Framo. New York: Harper & Row.
Framo, J. (1972) 'Symptoms from a Transactional Viewpoint.' In *Progress in Group and Family Therapy*, edited by C. Sager and H. Kaplan. New York: Bruner-Mazel.
Framo, J. (1976) 'Family of Origin as a Therapeutic Resource for Adults in Marital and Family Therapy – You Can and You Should Go Home Again.' *Family Process* 15, 193–210.
Frankl, V. (1963) *Man's Search for Meaning*. New York: Washington Square Press.
Goldstein, A. and Foa, B. (Eds) (1980) *Handbook of Behavioural Interventions – A Clinical Guide*. New York: John Wiley.
Gordon, T. (1970) *Parent Effectiveness Training*. New York: Plume Books.
Graham, H. (1980) 'Mothers' Accounts of Anger and Aggression Towards Their Babies.' In *Psychological Approaches to Child Abuse*, edited by N. Frude. London: Batsford Academic Press.

Greer, G. (1970) *The Female Eunuch*. St Albans, England: Paladin Books.
Gurman, A. J. and Kniskern, D. P. (1978) 'Research on Marital and Family Therapy – Progress, Perspective and Prospect.' In *Handbook of Psychotherapy and Behaviour Change*, 2nd edn, edited by Garfield, A. S. and Bergin, A. New York: John Wiley.
Halmos, P. (1965) *The Faith of the Counsellors*. London: Constable.
Hart, N. (1976) *When Marriage Ends*. London: Tavistock.
Hayley, J. (1959) 'An Interactional Description of Schizophrenia.' *Psychiatry* 22, 321–332.
Hayley, J. (1971) 'A Review of the Family Therapy Field.' In *Changing Families*, edited by J. Hayley. New York: Grune & Stratton.
Hayley, J. (1976) *Problem-solving Therapy*. San Francisco: Jossey-Bass.
Hess, A. K. (1980) *Psychotherapy Supervision – Theory, Research and Practice*. New York: John Wiley.
Hewitt, J. (1982) *Relaxation East and West – A Manual of Poised Living*. London: Rider.
Hill, B. (1958) 'On Being Rather than Doing in Psychotherapy.' *International Journal of Group Psychotherapy* 8, 115–122.
Home Office (1979) *Marriage Matters*. London: HMSO.
Hopson, B. and Scally, M. (1981) *Lifeskills Teaching*. Maidenhead: McGraw-Hill.
Illich, I. D. (1972) *Limits to Medicine – Medical Nemesis: The Expropriation of Health*. London: Calder & Boyars.
Jackson, D. D. (1957) 'The Question of Family Homeostasis.' *Psychiatric Quarterly* 31 (Supplement), 79–90.
Jacobson, N. S. (1977) 'Problem-solving and Contingency Contracting in the Treatment of Marital Discord.' *Journal of Consulting and Clinical Psychology* 45, 92–100.
Jones, S. L. (1980) *Family Therapy – A Comparison of Approaches*. Bowie, Md: Robert Brady.
Kaplan, H. I., Freedman, A. M. and Sadock, B. (1980) *Comprehensive Textbook of Psychiatry*, 3rd edn. Baltimore: Williams & Wilkins.
Kobasa, S. C. and Puccetti, M. (1983) 'Personality and Social Resources in Stress Resistance.' *Journal of Personality and Social Psychology* 45(4), 839–850.
Laing, R. D. (1970) *Knots*. London: Tavistock.
Laing, R. D. (1971) *The Politics of the Family*. London: Tavistock.
Laing, R. D. and Esterson, A. (1970) *Society, Madness and the Family*. Harmondsworth: Penguin.

Lange, A. J. and Jakubowski, P. (1976) *Responsible Assertive Behaviour – Cognitive and Behavioural Procedures for Trainers.* Champaign, Ill: Research Press.

Lazarus, R. S. (1978) 'The Stress and Coping Paradigm.' Mimeo of a paper presented at a conference on The Critical Evaluation of Behavioural Paradigms for Psychiatric Science (November), available from Professor R. S. Lazarus, University of California at Berkeley.

Lazarus, R. S. and Launier, R. (1982) 'Stress Related Transactions Between Person and Environment.' In *Perspectives in Interaction Psychology,* edited by L. A. Pervin and M. Lewis. New York: Plenum.

Liberman, R. P. and Roberts, J. (1976) 'Contingency Management of Neurotic Depression and Marital Disharmony.' In *Case Studies in Behaviour Therapy,* edited by H. J. Eysenck. London: Routledge & Kegan Paul.

Liebman, R., Minuchin, S. and Baker, L. (1974) 'An Integrated Treatment Program for Anorexia Nervosa.' *American Journal of Psychiatry* 131, 432–434.

Leonard, P. (1984) *Personality and Ideology – Towards a Materialist Understanding of the Individual.* London: Macmillan.

McGuire, M. and Sifnoes, D. (1970) 'Problem-solving in Psychotherapy.' *Psychiatric Quarterly* 44, 667–673.

Marsden, D. and Duff, E. (1975) *Workless – Some Unemployed Men and Their Families.* Harmondsworth: Penguin.

May, R. (1967) *Psychology and the Human Dilemma.* Princeton: Van Nostrand.

May, J. R. (1977) 'Psychophysiology of Self-regulated Thoughts.' *Behaviour Therapy* 8, 150–159.

Meichenbaum, D. (1977) *Cognitive Behaviour Modification.* New York: Plenum.

Mereness, D. A. (1968) 'Family Therapy – An Evolving Role for the Psychiatric Nurse.' *Perspectives in Psychiatric Care* 8, 256–259.

Millet, K. (1970) *Sexual Politics.* St Albans, England: Hart-Davis.

Minuchin, S. (1974) *Families and Family Therapy.* London: Tavistock.

Minuchin, S. and Fishman, H. C. (1981) *Family Therapy Techniques.* Cambridge, Mass.: Harvard University Press.

Minuchin, S., Rosman, B. and Baker, L. (1978) *Psychosomatic Families – Anorexia Nervosa in Context.* Cambridge, Mass.: Harvard University Press.

Moos, R. H. and Moos, B. S. (1976) 'A Typology of Family Social Environment.' *Social Psychiatry* 11, 51–58.

Munro, E. A., Manthei, R. J. and Small, J. J. (1983) *Counselling – A Skills Approach*. Wellington, New Zealand: Methuen.
Murgatroyd, S. (Ed.) (1980) *Helping the Troubled Child – Interprofessional Case Studies*. London: Harper & Row.
Murgatroyd, S. (1981) 'The "Threat" of the Counsellor.' *The Counsellor* 3(4), 13–21.
Murgatroyd, S. (1982) ' "Coping" and the Crisis Counsellor.' *British Journal of Guidance and Counselling* 10(2), 151–166.
Murgatroyd, S. (1983) 'Training for Crisis Counselling.' *British Journal of Guidance and Counselling* 11(2), 131–144.
Murgatroyd, S. (1984) 'Counselling Psychology.' In *Psychology Survey No. 5*, edited by H. Beloff and J. Nicholson. Leicester: British Psychological Society.
Murgatroyd, S. (1985) 'Dealing with an Acute Crisis in Marital Relationships.' In *Marital Therapy*, Vol. 2, edited by W. Dryden. London: Harper & Row.
Murgatroyd, S. and Apter, M. J. (1984) 'Eclectic Psychotherapy – A Structural Phenomenological Approach.' In *Individual Psychotherapy*, edited by W. Dryden. London: Harper & Row.
Murgatroyd, S. and Woolfe, R. (1982) *Coping with Crisis – Understanding and Helping People in Need*. London: Harper & Row.
Murgatroyd, S., Cade, B. and Shooter, M. (1985) 'Family and Relationship Counselling.' *British Journal of Guidance and Counselling* 12(1), 45–56.
Nelson-Jones, R. (1982) *The Theory and Practice of Counselling Psychology*. London: Holt-Saunders.
Nelson-Jones, R. (1983) *Practical Counselling Skills*. London: Holt-Saunders.
Nicholson, J. (1980) *Seven Ages*. London: Fontana.
O'Leary, K. D. and Turkewitz, M. (1978) 'Marital Therapy from a Behavioural Perspective.' In *Marriage and Marital Therapy*, edited by T. J. Paolino and B. S. McCrady. New York: Bruner-Mazel.
Oakley, A. (1976) *Housewife*. Harmondsworth: Penguin.
Olson, D. H., Sprenkle, D. H., and Russell, C. (1979) 'Circumplex Model of Marital and Family Systems.' *Family Process* 18, 2–28.
Open University (1982) *Parents and Teenagers*. Milton Keynes: Centre for Continuing Education/Open University Press.
Orford, J. (1980) 'The Domestic Context.' In *Psychological Problems – The Social Context*, edited by P. Feldman and J. Orford. London: John Wiley.

REFERENCES

Papp, P., Silverstein, O. and Carter, E. (1973) 'Family Sculpting in Preventive Work with Well-Families.' *Family Process* 12, 197–212.

Patterson, G. (1975) *Application of Social Learning to Family Life*. Champaign, Ill.: Research Press.

Patterson, G. R. and Reid, J. (1970) 'Reciprocity and Coercion – Two Facets of Social Systems.' In *Behaviour Modification in Clinical Psychology*, edited by C. Neuringer and J. Michael. New York: Appleton–Century–Crofts.

Patterson, G. R., Weiss, R. L. and Hops, H. (1977) 'Training in Marital Skills.' In *Handbook of Behaviour Modification and Behaviour Therapy*, edited by H. Leitenberg. Englewood Cliffs, N.J: Prentice Hall.

Pearlin, L. and Schooler, C. (1978) 'The Structure of Coping.' *Journal of Health and Social Behaviour* 18, 2–21.

Pelazzoli, M. S., Boscolo, L., Cecchin, G., and Prata, G. (1978) *Paradox and Counter-paradox*. New York: Aronson.

Perls, F. (1969) *Gestalt Therapy Verbatim*. New York: Bantam Books.

Pincus, L. and Dare, C. (1978) *Secrets in the Family*. London: Faber and Faber.

Puryear, D. A. (1975) *Helping People in Crisis*. San Francisco: Jossey-Bass.

Rachman, S. (1968) *Phobias – Their Nature and Control*. Springfield, Ill.: Charles C. Thomas.

Rachman, S. (1976) 'Observational Learning and Therapeutic Modelling.' In *The Theoretical and Experimental Basis of Behaviour Therapies*, edited by M. P. Feldman and A. Broadhurst. New York: John Wiley.

Rachman, S. and Wilson, G. T. (1980) *The Effects of Psychological Therapies*, 2nd edn. Oxford: Pergamon.

Rathus, S. A. and Nevid, J. S. (1977) *Behaviour Therapy – Strategies for Solving Problems in Living*. New York: Doubleday (Signet).

Raymond, J. (1984) *Teaching the Child with Special Needs*. London: Ward Lock.

Rogers, C. R. (1957) 'The Necessary and Sufficient Conditions of Therapeutic Personality Change.' *Journal of Consulting and Clinical Psychology* 21, 95–103.

Rogers, T. and Craighead, W. E. (1977) 'Physiological Responses to Self Statements.' *Cognitive Therapy Research* 1, 99–120.

Ross, J. (1979) 'The Identification of Marital Interaction.' *Marriage Guidance Newsletter*, December, 265–269.

Russell, C. (1979) 'Circumplex Model of Family Systems – Empirical Evaluation with Families.' *Family Process* 18, 29–45.

Satir, V. (1967) *Conjoint Family Therapy.* Palo Alto, Calif.: Science and Behaviour Books.

Schwartz, S. L. (1971) 'A Review of Crisis Intervention Programmes.' *Psychiatric Quarterly* **45**, 498–508.

Seeger, P. A. (1976) 'A Framework for Family Therapy.' *Journal of Psychiatric Nursing* **14**, 23–28.

Seligman, M. E. P. (1975) Helplessness – On Depression, Development and Death. San Francisco: W. H. Freeman.

Sheehy, G. (1977) *Passages.* New York: Bantam.

Skynner, R. (1976) *One Flesh – Separate Persons.* London: Constable.

Skynner, R. and Cleese, J. (1983) *Families and How to Survive Them.* London: Methuen.

Skynner, R., Cleese, J. and Strachan, A. (1983) 'Family Matters.' *Changes* **2**(1), 4–7.

Speck, R. V. and Attneave, C. (1971) 'Network Therapy.' In *The Book of Family Therapy,* edited by A. Ferber, M. Mendelsohn and A. Napier. Boston: Houghton-Mifflin.

Speck, R. V. and Rueveni, U. (1969) 'Network Therapy – A Developing Concept.' *Family Process* **8**, 182–191.

Speed, B. (1984) 'Family Therapy – An Update.' *Newsletter of the Association for Child Psychology and Psychiatry* **6**(1), 2–14.

Spivack, G. and Shure, M. B. (1974) *Social Adjustment of Young Children.* San Francisco: Jossey-Bass.

Sprenkle, D. and Olson, D. (1978) 'Circumplex Model of Marital Systems – Empirical Studies of Clinic and Non-clinic Couples.' *Journal of Marriage and Family Counseling* **4**, 59–74.

Storr, A. (1979) *The Art of Psychotherapy.* London: Secker and Warburg/Heinemann Medical Books.

Walrond-Skinner, S. (1976) *Family Therapy – The Treatment of Natural Systems.* London: Routledge & Kegan Paul.

Walrond-Skinner, S. (Ed.) (1981) *Developments in Family Therapy – Theories and Applications since 1948.* London: Routledge & Kegan Paul.

Watzlawick, P., Beavin, J. H. and Jackson, D. D. (1967) *Pragmatics of Human Communication.* New York: W. W. Norton.

Watzlawick, P., Weakland, J. H. and Fisch, R. (1974) *Principles of Problem Formation and Problem Resolution.* New York: W. W. Norton.

Whittaker, C. (1976) 'The Hindrance of Theory in Clinical Work.' In *Family Therapy – Theory and Practice,* edited by P. Guerin. New York: Gardner Press.

Willmott, P. and Young, M. (1960) *Family and Class in a London Suburb.* London: Routledge & Kegan Paul.
Windheuser, H. J. (1977) 'Anxious Mothers as Models for Coping with Anxiety.' *European Journal of Behavioural Analysis and Modification* 2, 39–58.
Winnicott, D. W. (1956) *The Family and Individual Development.* London: Tavistock.
Wolpe, J. (1973) *The Practice of Behaviour Therapy.* New York: Pergamon.
Woolfe, R. (1983) 'Counselling in a World of Crisis – Towards a Sociology of Counselling.' *International Journal for the Advancement of Counselling* 6, 167–176.
Wynne, L. C. (1971) 'Some Guidelines for Exploratory Conjoint Family Therapy. In *Changing Families*, edited by J. Hayley. New York: Grune & Stratton.
Young, M. and Willmott, P. (1957) *Family and Kinship in East London.* London: Routledge & Kegan Paul.
Yule, W. (1984) 'Child Behaviour Therapy in Britain, 1962–1982.' *Newsletter of the Association for Child Psychology and Psychiatry* 6(1), 15–20.

INDEX OF NAMES

Adlam, D., 3
Anderson, D. B., 8
Apter, M. J., 40, 87, 89
Attneave, C., 8

Baker, L., 39, 51
Bandura, A., 94
Barker, P., 8, 62, 66
Bateson, G., 36, 38
Beavin, J. H., 51, 62
Becvar, R. J., 110
Berenson, B. G., 127
Bettelheim, B., 19
Boscolo, L., 38, 44
Boszormenyi-Nagy, I., 66
Bowen, M., 142
Boy, A. V., 4
Brandon, S., 129
Bulkeley, R., 87

Cade, B., 44, 154
Carkhuff, R. R., 127
Carmody, T. P., 101
Carter, E., 53
Cecchin, G., 38, 44
Cleese, J., 25
Clement, J. A., 8
Cochrane, A. L., 2
Cooper, D., 20
Copermann, C. D., 109
Cox, M., 153
Coyne, J. C., 154
Craighead, W. E., 111

Dare, C., 64–68
David, J., 69
Dobash, R., 29
Dobash, R. E., 29
Dryden, W., 111
Duck, S., 154
Duhl, B. S., 53
Duhl, F. J., 53
D'Zurilla, T. J., 105

Eaton, M., 69
Ellis, A., 111–112
Erikson, E. H., 31
Erwin, E., 4
Esterson, A., 20
Eysenck, H. J., 1, 88, 91

Faulder, C., 23
Fisch, R., 51, 62
Fishman, H. C., 60
Fitzpatrick, M. A., 154
Foa, B., 116
Folkman, S., 31, 136
Foucault, M., 86
Framo, J., 65–66, 69, 81
Frankl, V., 31, 62
Freedman, A. M., 8

Goldfried, M. R., 105
Goldstein, A., 116
Gordon, T., 98, 110
Graham, H., 9
Greer, G., 18
Gurman, A. J., 154

INDEX OF NAMES

Halmos, P., 3
Hart, N., 124
Hayes, J., 152
Hayley, J., 6, 38, 62, 105
Henriques, J., 3
Hess, A. K., 149
Hewitt, J., 93, 132
Hill, B., xv
Hops, H., 86
Hopson, B., 115, 152

Illich, I. D., 2

Jackson, D. D., 16, 51, 62
Jacobson, N. S., 104
Jakubowski, P., 98
Jones, S. L., 52, 62, 66, 89, 90

Kantor, D., 53
Kaplan, H. I., 8
Kniskern, D. P., 154
Kobasa, S. C., 127, 136

Laing, R. D., 20, 26, 38
Lange, A. J., 98
Launier, R., 9, 125
Lazarus, R. S., 9, 30–31, 125, 136
Leonard, P., xii, 3
Liberman, R. P., 101–103
Liebman, R., 51
Lock, A., 154

Manthei, R. J., 140
May, R., 4
May, J. R., 111
McCall, G., 154
McGuire, M., 109
Meichenbaum, D., 112
Mereness, D. A., 8
Millet, K., 18
Minuchin, S., 16, 19, 34, 39, 41, 44–46, 49–51, 60, 87, 136
Moos, B. S., 30
Moos, R. H., 30
Munro, E. A., 140
Murgatroyd, S., 1, 9, 27, 40, 45–46, 73, 87, 99, 118–119, 122, 125, 129, 130, 133, 136, 147, 149, 154

Nevid, J. S., 93, 95
Nelson-Jones, R., 151, 153
Nicholson, J., 25

O'Leary, K. D., 110
Oakley, A., 18
Olson, D. H., 41
Orford, J., 29–30

Papp, P., 53
Patterson, G., 86, 89, 100
Pearlin, L., 127, 129, 136
Pelazzoli, M. S., 34, 38, 44
Perls, F., 4
Peterson, M., 69
Pincus, L., 64–68
Pine, G. P., 4
Prata, G., 38, 44
Pucetti, M., 127, 136
Puryear, D. A., 121–122

Rachman, S., 86, 94–96
Rathus, S. A., 93, 95
Raymond, J., 86, 94
Reid, J., 100
Roberts, J., 101–103
Rogers, C. R., 1
Rogers, T., 111
Rose, N., 3
Rosman, B., 39
Ross, J., 83
Rueveni, U., 8
Russell, C., 41

Sadock, B., 8
Salfield, 3
Sahami, V., 87
Satir, V., 16
Scally, M., 115
Schooler, C., 127, 129, 136
Schwartz, S. L., 133, 135
Seeger, P. A., 8
Seligman, M. E. P., 88
Sheehy, G., 24
Shooter, M., 44, 46, 154
Shure, M. D., 109
Sifnoes, D., 109
Silverstein, O., 53
Skynner, R., 25, 68
Small, J. J., 140
Smith, K. C. P., 89
Speck, R. V., 8
Speed, B., 6, 68, 85
Spivack, G., 109
Sprenkle, D. H., 41

Storr, A., 7, 79
Strachan, A., 25

Turkewitz, M., 110

Venn, C., 3

Walerdine, V., 3
Walrond-Skinner, S., 6, 69, 147
Watzlawick, P., 34, 51, 62
Weakland, J. H., 51, 62
Weiss, R. L., 86
Whittaker, C., 116
Willmott, P., 19
Wilson, G. T., 86, 95
Windheuser, H. J., 98
Winnicott, D. W., 65
Wolpe, J., 90, 93
Woolfe, R., xii, 3, 9, 27, 44, 46, 73, 99, 118–119, 130, 133
Wynne, L. C., 7

Young, M., 19
Yule, W., 85

INDEX OF SUBJECTS

acceptance, 95, 134
accident, 128
accidental, (or incidental), learning, 89
active listening, 139
adaptability, 34, 39, 44, 49–50, 58
adaptive learning, 88
adolescent (ce), 71, 119
adult, 68, 76–77, 79
affection, 103
aggression/aggressive, 67, 78–80, 83–85, 98
aggressive drive, 70
anarchic, 78
anger, 61, 66, 69, 75–76, 82–84, 91, 99
anticipatory coping, 127–128
anxiety, 71–72, 92–93, 96
assertiveness training, 92, 98–101, 110, 115, 132, 144
assessment/evaluation, 62, 86, 100, 111, 134, 145
attitude, 64, 69, 78
attribution of credit, 62
Aunts and Uncles, 57, 142
aversion therapy, 117
awareness, 26, 28, 78

bedwetting, 86, 145–146
behavioural analysis, 90–93, 102
behavioural contracts (elements of), 104; see also contracts
behaviour modification, 92
belief 64, 126; see also irrational belief
bereavement, 10, 45
blocking, 59
blame, 67, 123, 134

body, 10, 110
boundaries, 33–34, 52, 54, 147–149
brainstorming, 106–107, 134
buffer coping, 129–130

cancer, 9
career choice, 1
'Catch 22', 36, 88, 93
capitalism, 3–4, 18; see also ideology
change strategy, 47
chaotic (families), 45–47, 49, 136
child/children, 7, 21, 23, 53, 71, 76, 83, 89, 131
child abuse, 9
childbirth, 96–97
childcare, 47
childhood, 80
childish, 83
clergy, 8
client (use of terminology about), xvi, 2–3, 73
client withdrawal, 75–76
clinical psychologist, xiii, 69, 86; see also psychologist
coalition, 53, 54
cognitive behaviour therapy, 92, 110–115, 144
cohesion, 29, 39, 44, 49–50, 58
collusion, 61, 67, 101, 148
communication (s), 6, 33–34, 57–58, 63, 147
    patterns of within families, 35–51, 60, 99, 138, 144, 146, 148
    rules of, 58

skills training, 92, 98, 103, 110
community, 8–10, 48, 71, 152
community nurse, xiii
concreteness, xv, 107, 132, 139, 150
conditioning, 88
confidence, 59
conflict, 16–17, 21, 54, 59–60, 65, 67, 75, 77, 82, 98, 109, 124
confrontation, 60, 129, 131, 141
connected (families), 41, 43
consciousness, 67, 70
contingency contracting, 88, 92, 100–104, 129, 144, 153
contract, 93, 100–101, 133, 143–145, 151
control, 83
   as a shaper of crisis experience, 15, 126
   coping mechanisms, 15, 30
   process of, 12, 120–121, 125
   skills, 136–137
   strategies, 31, 88, 119–120, 126–132, 136–137
   styles, 31
   tactics, 31, 126
   with change, 45
Coping with Crisis, Research and Training Group, xi
counselling, 1, 32, 79
counsellor (s), xv, 1, 3, 4, 73, 81, 85, 117, 139, 150
counter-transference, 74–75
covert-conditioning, 92
covert modelling, 96
creativity, 126
crisis, 108–109, 125–126
   a subjective phenomenon, 118–119
   features of, 119, 121–124
   triggers for, 119
cross-cultural counselling, 147
C.R.U.S.E., 10

daughter, 42, 90, 98–99, 145
decision-making, 106–109, 134, 143
decision-making skills, 132
death, 69, 108, 119
defence mechanisms, 72, 79
definition of the situation, 56
denial, 126
dependence/dependent, 73, 83
depression, 40, 42, 88, 101, 145–146, 150
desire for children, 72
desires, 66, 81

despair, 31
detatched (families), 40–42, 49
detatchment, 148
developmental counselling, 127
discipline, 53
disowned feelings/parts of self, 79–80
dislike, 75
disruptive behaviour, 89
distress definitions of, 10, 13
   nature of, 11–13, 29
   origins, 11–13, 15
divorce, 21–24, 27, 123
doctor, xiii, 1, 5, 32, 58, 61, 86, 140–141
dominance/dominant, 67, 80, 83
drama-therapy, 53
drinking/alcohol, 96, 122

earlier childhood relationships, 67–69
eclectic (ism), 85, 87, 147
educational psychologist, 58, 86, 94, 98, 141; see also psychologist
Education Welfare Officer, 58, 86
ego, 71–73
ejaculation, 93
emotional discharge, 150
emotional experiences (typifying distress), 12
empathy, xv, 57, 81, 87, 90, 132, 139
encopresis, 87
enmeshed (families), 39, 41, 49, 52
equilibrium, 16–17, 20, 83–84, 135
erection, 61
examination, 111
expectation (s), 64

family (functions of), 16
family life skills, 115–116
fantasy, 66, 68, 84
fatalism, 131
father, 7, 42, 78, 98
fear (s), 64, 67, 101
feedback, 139
fight or flight, 83
fit (between person and environment), 120, 125
flexibility, 26, 30, 34, 47, 136
flooding, 92
Freudian model of personality, 69–73
frustration, 75, 150

games, 38, 78, 145
generation of alternatives, 106
genuineness, xv, 57, 81, 87, 90, 115, 132, 139–140
glue-sniffing, 54
goals, 62, 102, 113, 124
grandparents, 21, 34, 53–55, 57, 142
grief, 121
grief-work, 10, 27
guilt, 71

hardy, 127–128
handicap, 27, 31; *see also* mental handicap and physical handicap
Health Visitor, xiii, 32, 58, 96, 141
heart disease, 2
helper, as parent and adult, 76–77
 as teacher/educator, 130–133, 135–136
 burnout, 4
 questions to be asked in helping, 11–14, 77–78, 140–143, 151
 self of, 74
 terminology about, xv–xvi, 3, 73
Helper's, own needs, 4
 specific tasks in a crisis, 133, 135
Helping, ending of relationship, 138, 151–154
 establishing a relationship, 138, 140–145
 in crisis work, 76, 124–125
 in problem solving, 105
 procedures (practices), 52–53, 56, 59, 87
 relationship (characters of), xv, 62, 87
 sustaining a relationship, 138, 145–150
helpless (ness), 88, 119, 126–127
hierarchy, 58
hierarchy of behaviour, 95
homework assignment/task, 95, 96, 144
holistic, 14
homosexual, 37, 74, 147
humanistic, xii, 78, 117
husband, 61, 71, 83, 97, 101, 103, 121, 145
hypothesis, 52, 58, 146–148, 150, 153; *see also* working assumption

Id, 69–70, 72–73
ideology, 20, 33, 73; *see also* capitalism
illness, 9, 27, 31, 37, 40, 43, 45, 106, 108, 119, 131
implicit rules, 57
implosive therapy, 92
incest, 70

independent, 83
individualised approach to helping, 2–4, 64
inner life/inner world, 64–68
insight, 58, 64, 78, 79, 81
integrative tendency, 65
integrity, 31
interaction, 6–7, 30, 33, 37, 49–50, 58, 68, 70
interlocking patterns, 68
internal mental processes, 86
interpretation, 79
invalid, 67
irrational beliefs, 111–115, 130

Judgement (making of) 109

levels of intervention, 7–13, 33
life cycle (of the family), 24–25, 28–29, 32
live modelling, 96
loss, 27, 69, 88, 121; *see also* grief
love/affection, 101

maladaptive learning, 88–90
maladjustment, 65–66
manipulation, 62
marital fit, 80
marital relationships, xiii, 38, 67, 71, 81, 110, 119, 128, 154
Marriage Guidance Counsellor, xiii, 61, 83
masculine behaviour/emotions, 77
mental handicap, 3, 86; *see also* handicap
midwife, 141
modelling, 92, 95–98, 100; *see also* live, symbolic, and covert modelling
modelling of behaviour, 77
mother, 7, 42, 99
mothers and babies, 9
motivation, 25, 66, 70, 126, 141, 143

need (individualising of), 2–4
needs, 66–67
 developmental, 1
 educational, 1
 transitional, 1
 vocational, 1
negative feelings (expression of), 25–27, 75
negotiation, 133, 143–144, 151
nervous breakdown, 122
network of behaviours, 89
network therapy, 8
nightmare, 96

non-directive facilitation, 76
non-verbal behaviour, 110
nosebleed, 43
N.S.P.C.C., 141
nurses, 5, 32

Object Relations Approach, 68
observation, 60, 62, 145
oedipus complex, 68
one-parent families, 23
open communication, 26
Open University, xi, 116
operant conditioning, 95
orgasm, 92–94
Oxford Dictionary (definition of distress), 10

paradox (paradoxical intention), 61–62, 153
parent (s), 65, 76, 83, 89, 90, 95
parental, 83
parent effectiveness training, 110
parental figure, 76
parental relationships (re-enactment of), 68
passive/passivity, 78, 82
persecutor, 148
personal development (through marriage), 22
personal identity, 123
phases of helping, 57–58
phobia, 94, 98
physical handicap see also handicap, 3, 86, 120
physical violence, 9, 21, 97
positive comparison, 129
positive connotation, 43–44, 60
premature ejaculation, 61
premature termination of helping relationship, 152
privatised families, 19–20
Probation Service/Officer 58, 86, 140
problem-solving, 92
problem-solving skills, 105–109, 127–129, 134
projection (s), 64, 67–68, 79–82, 123, 134, 147
psychiatrist (psychiatry), 1, 8
psychoanalytical tradition/approach, 64–65, 68, 74, 76, 79, 82, 84
psychologist, 61, 140–141; see also educational psychologist/clinical psychologist

psychosomatic, 40
punishment, 70

rape, 10, 119, 128
rational emotive imagery, 114
reactional restructuring, 112–115
reaction and response (difference between), 76
reality focus, 148
referral, 152–153
reframing, 44, 111, 126, 130
reinforcement, 88–90, 101, 103–104
rejection, 152
relationship problem, 76
relaxation (progressive), 92–95
repression, 72, 81–82, 126, 147
research, 154
response, 88, 90, 94
rigidity, 30, 46–49, 78, 136
risk, 119, 126, 154
rituals, 145, 147
role of the helper in psychoanalytical tradition, 73–79
role of the helper (re family communication system), 57–63
role system, 63
roles, 33–34, 39, 50–52, 56, 58, 147
role play, 100–114
rules (within families), 33, 35–53, 58, 145, 147

sadness, 69, 82
Samaritans, 32
scapegoat, 66
schizophrenic, 38
school, 40–41, 47, 65, 69
scientific method, 86, 92, 116
sculpting, 53
second marriages, 23
selective ignoring, 130
self-critical scrutiny/awareness, 63, 149
self disclosure, 141
self-identity, 30
self pity, 123
separated (families), 41
sex/sexual, 65, 74, 128, 145–146
sex talk, 92–94
sexual attraction, 67, 78
    behaviour/activity/advances, 48, 54, 72, 75, 92–94
    division of labour, 18–19, 21–22, 28–29

drive, 70, 82
problems, 61, 76, 82
relationships (extra-marital), 71
sexuality, 26, 72, 75
shy and withdrawn, 98
smoking, 41
social engineering, 19
social policy, 2, 11, 152
social skills, 1, 6, 78, 88
social work (er), xiii, 1, 32, 58, 86, 101, 140
son, 66, 95, 145
spirit, 10
spontaneous/spontaneity, 78, 83
stammering (stutter), 43, 61, 145
standard family, 48
status passage, 123–124
stimulus, 88, 90, 94
stress management, 130–132
strict moral background, 67
stuck feelings, 76, 150
sub-groups, 50, 119, 126, 140, 146–147, 152
subconscious, 67
submissive, 83
suicide, 42, 122
superego, 70–73
supervision, 149–150
support networks, 123–124, 126–127
swearing, 91
symptom (s), 43, 62, 74, 88
symptom carrier, 55–57, 60
symbol, 42, 53, 56, 73, 90
symbolic modelling, 96
system, 6, 16, 20, 33–34, 68, 74, 82, 123
systematic desensitization, 92–95
systems theory, 16, 87

teacher, 32, 86
temper tantrums, 90
therapist (psychotherapist), 73–74, 111, 135
thinking processes, 12
time, 124, 131, 142, 144
transaction (between person and environment), 31
Transactional Analysis, 76
transference, 64, 74–75, 79, 81, 84, 132, 147
transition, 123–124, 126–127
transition learning, 152
truancy, 86

trust, 62, 105, 139

unconscious, 67, 70, 72, 89
unemployment, 10–11, 15, 21, 27–29, 44, 46, 106, 118, 123
unrealistic expectations, 76, 143

values, 126
verification, 106
victim, 38–39, 68, 88, 106, 148
video, 110
voice, (tone of) 110

warmth, xv, 57, 81, 87, 90, 95, 132, 134, 139
wife, 21, 22, 39, 61, 83, 97, 101, 103, 121, 145
wishes, 64
withdrawal, 131
women (role in the family), 17–18
working assumption, 58; see also hypothesis